Win

The 1992 Summer Olympic Games in Barcelona, Spain, were a bigger success for gymnast Shannon Miller than even she could have imagined. She had won five Olympic medals! At 4' 6" and 69 pounds, she was the shortest and lightest U.S. athlete at the Games. But she had won more medals than any of her teammates.

Shannon returned to the United States as a star. She was made honorary mayor of Oklahoma City and honorary governor of Oklahoma! She was given a new car — even though she was 15 and still too young to drive.

Suddenly, Shannon was receiving more than 100 fan letters a week and being showered with gifts from admirers. When a team of Olympic and world-champion gymnasts gave a series of exhibitions in 23 U.S. cities, Shannon received the loudest cheers.

But Shannon's fans hadn't seen the best of her yet.

Shannon Miller is certainly one of the most exciting athletes in the world today. Now read all about her life, and the lives of seven other extraordinary women athletes. Find out about how they got their start, the challenges they've faced, their dreams, and the heart and determination that has made each of them a winner!

Winning Women

By Fred McMane and Cathrine Wolf

A *Sports Illustrated For Kids* Book

BANTAM BOOKS

TORONTO • NEW YORK • LONDON • SYDNEY • AUCKLAND

Winning Women by Fred McMane and Cathrine Wolf

A Bantam Book/March 1995

Sports Illustrated For Kids and **KIDS** are registered trademarks of Time Inc.
Sports Illustrated For Kids Books are published in cooperation with Bantam
Doubleday Dell Publishing Group, Inc. under license from Time Inc.

Cover and interior design by Miriam Dustin.
Front cover photographs by Dave Black; back cover photographs by Shaun
Botterill/Allsport (Julie Krone) and Dave Black (Gail Devers).

ISBN 0-553-48290-4

Published simultaneously in the United States and Canada

Bantam books are published by Bantam Books, a division of Bantam Doubleday
Dell Publishing Group, Inc. Its trademark, consisting of the words "Bantam
Books" and the portrayal of a rooster, is Registered in the U.S. Patent and
Trademark Office and in other countries. Marca Registrada. Bantam Books,
1540 Broadway, New York, NY 10036

Printed in the United States of America

CWO 10 9 8 7 6 5 4 3 2 1

Table of Contents

Oksana Baiul

T he story of Oksana Baiul is a modern-day fairy tale. It is part Cinderella, part Hans Brinker, and part Aladdin. It could even begin, "Once upon a time. . . ."

It is the story of a poor little girl who had to overcome many hardships. Her father and her coach abandoned her. Her mother and her grandparents died. She was all alone at the age of 13.

But, like Hans Brinker, Oksana had a pair of ice skates, and she loved to use them. Her love of skating helped her overcome the difficult times in her life. And by the time she was 16, she had become a queen — of figure skating.

★

Oksana Baiul [AHK-zan-ah by-OOL] was born on November 16, 1977, in Dnepropetrovsk, a city in Ukraine. Ukraine — a

OKSANA BAIUL

Born:
November 16, 1977
Birthplace:
Dnepropetrovsk, Ukraine (then part of the Soviet Union)
Height: 5' 3"
Weight: 95 pounds

Oksana, in a figure-skating exhibition after her gold-medal performance at the 1994 Olympics, is the youngest champion since Sonja Henie.

DAVE BLACK

country about the size of Texas — is in Eastern Europe, and was part of the Soviet Union until 1991. When Oksana was 2, her parents separated. She lived with her mother, Marina, and her mother's parents. She didn't see her father, Sergei, again for 11 years.

Mrs. Baiul was a great influence on her daughter's life. She was a French teacher, and she impressed upon Oksana the importance of hard work.

Oksana was a chubby child, and when she was 3 ½, her mother and grandfather wanted to enroll her in ballet school. They felt that ballet dancing would help her lose some baby fat while teaching her poise and grace. But the local ballet school would not take any children younger than 7.

Oksana's grandfather suggested she try figure skating as a way of becoming fit and preparing for ballet. Figure skating is popular in Ukraine, which has a northern climate and takes great pride in its winter sports.

The little girl took to the sport at once. She was a natural on the ice, easily learning jumps, spins, and other moves. At the age of 5, she began to train with Stanislav Korytek [COR-ah-tek], one of the best skating coaches in the Soviet Union.

"When I was 7, I won my first competition, so I decided to stay in figure skating," Oksana remembers. Ballet was a forgotten subject.

Oksana was 10 years old when her world began to crumble. Her grandfather died in 1987 and her grandmother died a year later. Then, in 1991, Marina Baiul was diagnosed as having ovarian cancer, a form of cancer that strikes the female reproductive organs. After a brief illness, Mrs. Baiul died. She was 36 years old.

Oksana was in shock. Suddenly, at the age of 13, she had no family. Even now, Oksana often breaks into tears at the mention of her mother's name.

Oksana's father attended her mother's funeral, but Oksana refused to speak to him. For years, she found it difficult to talk about him, and to this day, father and daughter have nothing to do with each other.

Homeless, Oksana was taken in by Coach Korytek. For a time, she also lived with a friend of her mother's. Oksana felt lonely and abandoned — except at the skating rink. The hours of practice kept her busy and the competitions gave her something to look forward to.

"It helps me forget," Oksana once explained. "It helps me get over the pain."

While Oksana's life was in ruins, her country was also falling apart. The Union of Soviet Socialist Republics,

Winning Ways

At age 15, Oksana became the second youngest skater ever to win a world championship. At 16, she won an Olympic gold medal in Lillehammer, Norway. (1994).

as the Soviet Union was officially known, was a huge nation. Beginning in 1991, the republics that had made up the union broke away to become 15 independent countries.

There were many changes in these countries that were confusing and unsettling to the people who lived there. There was a shortage of food, supplies, and jobs. People went to other countries to look for work.

One of those people was Coach Korytek. In 1992, while Oksana was away at a skating competition, her skating coach left Ukraine to take a job in Toronto, Ontario, Canada. "He called me afterward to tell me, and I understood his position," Oksana says. "Everyone wants to eat."

But Coach Korytek had not totally abandoned his prized pupil. He had contacted another famous skating coach, Galina Zmievskaya *[zim-YEV-sky-ya]* about working with Oksana.

Coach Zmievskaya did more than that! She took Oksana home to live in her apartment in Odessa, a large seaport city 12 hours by train from Dnepropetrovsk.

There, Oksana shared a room with Coach

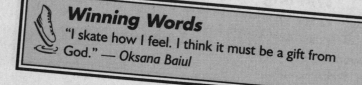

Winning Words
"I skate how I feel. I think it must be a gift from God." — *Oksana Baiul*

Zmievskaya's 12-year-old daughter, Galya. Coach Zmievskaya's husband, mother, and 19-year-old daughter, Nina, also lived in the apartment (although Nina would soon move out). The family pets, a dog and a cockatoo, also lived there. The apartment had just three rooms and was very crowded!

Oksana and Galya became fast friends. They both loved rap music, teddy bears, and candy bars. Back in a loving home, Oksana enjoyed being a kid again. When she laughed, which was more often, it rocked the room.

"We have fun together, and when the music is too loud, we have headaches together," said Oksana's coach. "The atmosphere at home is always jolly."

Coach Zmievskaya also trained Viktor Petrenko, the 1992 Olympic men's figure-skating champion. Viktor was a frequent visitor to the Zmievskaya household because he was engaged to marry Nina. Viktor became like a brother to Oksana and was to do for her what the genie did for Aladdin: make her wishes come true.

"The first time I see Oksana, I see her skates," Viktor once recalled. "I see that the skates are old and I ask Oksana about them. She tells me she has been wearing the same blades for four years — that is four years with no new blades! I see her skating outfit and it is old, and I ask her about her fabric and she tells me she has no fabric. I did not know it then, but Oksana had nothing for skating — but nothing in her life, too."

Viktor and Coach Zmievskaya purchased new

skating boots, blades, and a skate-sharpening machine for Oksana. Viktor gave her the extra fabric from his skating outfits so she could make a dress in which to perform. He watched over her and served as her interpreter at skating competitions. "Her life was just beginning," Viktor said, "and we just wanted to help."

Although Oksana had few of the material things you need to skate, she had plenty of the things money can't buy: energy, dedication, grace, personality, and talent. But that wasn't what made Viktor and Coach Zmievskaya want to help. "When I saw her skate myself, I saw she had a talent," said Viktor. "My coach and I did not know how much talent she had, you must understand; we did not know she would become a champion. But most of all she interested me as a person."

Oksana's first taste of senior-level competition came soon after she moved to Odessa. She won the 1993 Ukrainian National Championships, even though many of the skaters were four or five years older than she was. In her first major international competition, the European Championships, in January 1993, she finished second to Surya Bonaly of France.

★

The crowds who watched Oksana perform quickly fell in love with her and she with them. She has soft green eyes and often wears her hair in a ponytail. Her smile can light up a darkened arena, and she is very emotional, capable of crying at a moment's notice even when she is very happy.

Despite her youth, Oksana has the elegant style of a mature woman on the ice. It is what sets her apart from the other skaters. Not surprisingly, her favorite skater is Jill Trenary, a three-time U.S. champion and 1990 world gold medalist. "She's an example of femininity," says Oksana. "Like a real woman. I try to show feminine skating. It is supposed to be figure skating."

Although small at 5' 3" and 95 pounds, Oksana looks much bigger on the ice because of her expressive arms and the unusual flexibility of her arms and hips. She is a competent jumper, but jumps are not what she does best. With her swanlike grace, Oksana is a ballet dancer on the ice. And like the best dancers, she gives the impression that the melody flows from her body rather than that she is reacting to the music.

Two months after the European Championships, Oksana competed at the 1993 World Championships, in Prague, Czech Republic. It was only her fourth appearance ever outside the former Soviet Union. Few people in the skating world had ever heard of her.

Cool Facts

Oksana has a passion for pizza and candy. She also loves stuffed animals and carries several with her when she travels. Her favorite movies are *Home Alone 2*, *The Bodyguard*, and *Beauty and the Beast*.

This would be the biggest performance of Oksana's life so far. But things didn't go smoothly. Viktor had bought her new skates, but she had not had time to try them out. She had to use old, crooked skates that had been handed down to her by a male skater in Ukraine.

Then, at practice, Oksana crashed into the boards around the rink! She injured disks in her back and neck. (Disks are the cushions between the vertebrae, which are the little bones that make up the spine.) But Oksana would not let these things bother her when it came time to perform.

After her name is announced, Oksana likes to stand in the corner of the rink for a few moments. When she is ready, she skates to the center of the ice to begin her routine. "I listen to my skates," she once explained. "They tell me when it's time to go out there."

In Prague, Oksana's skates spoke beautifully.

How It Works

In singles skating, men and women each perform two different programs. The short program must be 2 minutes, 40 seconds long, and is performed to music selected by the skater. Each skater's routine must contain eight moves: three jumps, three spins, and two footwork moves. The free-skating program, which lasts 4 minutes for women and 4 ½ for men, lets a skater be creative. Skaters select their own music and design their own routines to show off their athletic and artistic abilities.

Oksana was in second place after the short program, behind Nancy Kerrigan of the United States. But Nancy turned in a poor performance in the free-skating program, placing ninth, and dropped to fifth overall.

Now the competition came down to Oksana and Surya Bonaly. Surya was the superior jumper, able to leap higher than any woman in the competition, but Oksana was more poised and natural on the ice.

Wearing a bright blue outfit, 15-year-old Oksana electrified the audience and impressed the nine judges. She became the first woman from the former Soviet Union to win a singles figure-skating world championship and the youngest world champion in the sport since Sonja Henie in 1927.

When she learned that she had won, Oksana began weeping. She turned to her coach and said, "These tears are God's kisses from my mother in heaven."

★

Some skating experts and fans wondered if Oksana's victory at Prague had been a fluke. After all, she had not had much international experience. The 1994 Winter Olympics were less than a year away. They were not convinced that Oksana had the talent and poise to win again.

It looked as if the doubters might be right when Oksana performed at Skate America, in Dallas, Texas, in October. (Skate America is the largest international figure-skating competiton held in the United States.)

Oksana made several mistakes, falling on two triple

jumps and failing to land another jump. She won the competition only because her main rivals, including Surya Bonaly, performed even worse.

As the Olympics approached, the pressure on 16-year-old Oksana began to build. Then, suddenly, all of the pressure and attention shifted to two of her top rivals, Nancy Kerrigan and Tonya Harding of the United States.

Nancy and Tonya had both become involved in a big news story. While practicing at the U.S. Championships, Nancy was clubbed on the knee by a man. When the case was investigated, Tonya was connected to the attack. The police tried to piece together enough evidence to charge Tonya with a crime, but it took time. Meanwhile, Tonya was allowed to compete at the 1994 Winter Olympics in Lillehammer, Norway.

A figure-skating competition consists of two parts: a short, or technical program, and a long, or free-skate program *(see How It Works, page 14)*. The short program counts for one third of the final score and the long program two thirds.

When the Olympic competition began, Nancy looked to be at her best. She won the short program and had a strong long program that she felt would bring her the gold medal on the final night of competition. Oksana also performed well. She wore a black skating dress and skated a sassy routine to flamenco (a form of Spanish dance) music, to finish the short program in second place.

Oksana's supporters were also confident. "She

skated to her potential," Viktor said after Oksana's program. "And she is more at home with her free program."

But things had never come easily for Oksana in her young life and that wasn't about to change. On the day before the long program, Oksana went to the skating arena to practice. She took the ice along with five other skaters, and began practicing her jumps. Suddenly there was a collision! Oksana and skater Tanja Szewczenko of Germany crashed into each other.

Oksana suffered a cut right leg and a sore back. There was concern over whether she would be able to skate in the free program. But Oksana was determined not to miss this chance.

There were 24 skaters competing for the gold medal that night in Lillehammer. Both Nancy and Oksana would skate late in the evening, after most of the other skaters had performed.

Nancy skated before Oksana and performed beautifully. She jumped into the lead. Then it was Oksana's

Notable Quote
"This girl has had hard experiences. But she is soft. She is unusually good. She cannot do evil. People feel this and they love her. God gives many performers physical talent. He usually forgets to give them the soul of an artist. He gave Oksana everything."
— Galina Zmievskaya, Oksana's coach

turn. Before going onto the ice, she was given two injections to stop the pain from her fall. Then, she summoned all of her courage.

Skating to a medley of Broadway show tunes, Oksana presented a program that was artistic and dynamic. She skated a nearly flawless routine and even risked an extra triple jump near the end of the program.

In a very close decision, the judges ruled that Oksana's performance was better than Nancy's and awarded her the gold medal. Five of the judges placed Oksana first and four of them put Nancy in first place. Oksana's margin of victory was the slimmest in Olympic figure-skating history!

One judge, Britta Lindgren of Sweden, said the

TRAILBLAZER: SONJA HENIE

Sonja Henie of Norway won three Olympic gold medals and 10 straight world championships in women's figure skating. She won her first world title at the age of 14, and her first Olympic gold medal at 15. She skated in her first Olympics, in 1924, when she was 11! Sonja changed figure skating, introducing style and athleticism to the sport. She was the first to wear short skating skirts and white boots, and the first woman to do jumps regularly during her routine. Sonja later became a movie star in the United States.

decision was the most difficult she had faced in 30 years as a judge. She explained the difference between the two skaters this way:

"When Oksana presents a program, it is really coming from the heart, the inside," said Judge Lindgren. "To me, she's an artist on the ice. Nancy's a little more cold as a skater. She has a nice presentation, but it's not really coming from the inside."

★

It is still early in the story for Oksana. In the fall of 1994, she moved to the United States to live and train in Simsbury, Connecticut, the site of a new Olympic-size skating center. Coach Zmievskaya, Viktor, and Nina have also moved to Simsbury.

Oksana certainly is no longer a poor little girl. She has made a lot of money from endorsing products. She has been performing on a professional tour, and a movie based on her life is planned. She intends to continue competitive skating at least until after the 1998 Olympics.

Off the ice, Oksana still has the same kind of enthusiasm for life that she demonstrates in her performances. "She loves everything," says U.S. skating coach Linda Leaver, who once accompanied Oksana on an exhibition tour. "She loves staying in the hotels. She loves the food. She loves the fans. She loves the bus rides. And she loves to perform."

So far, Oksana's life has read like a fairy tale. Will she live happily ever after? She will certainly try! ★

Gail Devers

In 1990, Gail Devers, one of the fastest runners in women's track and field, could barely walk. She had been suffering from a mysterious illness for nearly two years.

Gail had been one of the favorites in the women's 100-meter hurdles at the 1988 Summer Olympic Games in Seoul, South Korea. But when the time came to race, her body simply was not up to the job.

The discovery that Gail had a disease was only the beginning of her problems, however. Part of the treatment Gail received for the illness caused her feet to swell so badly that she could not walk. For a time, she feared that she would never be able to walk again. Her parents moved in with her to help. They had to carry her whenever she had to go to the bathroom.

But Gail refused to be defeated. She worked hard and made one of the great-

GAIL DEVERS
Born: November 19, 1966
Birthplace: Seattle, Washington
Height: 5' 4"
Weight: 115 pounds

Gail Devers, here training at the hurdles, bounced back from a severe illness to become an Olympic gold medalist and world champion.

est comebacks in the history of sports. By the summer of 1992, Gail was standing on the medals platform at the Summer Olympics in Barcelona, Spain, with a gold medal around her neck. She had won the women's 100-meter dash. The woman who couldn't walk had earned the title "the world's fastest woman."

★

It was a long road to Barcelona from San Diego, California, where Gail grew up. Her father, Reverend Larry Devers, is the associate minister of a Baptist church. Her mother, Alabe, was a teacher's aide at an elementary school. She has a brother named Parenthesis. (Yes, just like the curved lines that surround this sentence!)

"We were a _Leave It to Beaver_ family," Gail recalls. "We had picnics, rode bikes, and played touch football together. We did Bible studies together. My father and brother played guitar together."

Although 14 months younger than Parenthesis, Gail often kept her brother from getting into trouble.

Winning Ways

Gail won a gold medal in the 100-meter dash at 1992 Summer Olympics. She won the 100-meter dash and the 100-meter hurdles at 1993 world championships. She holds the U.S. record for the 100-meter hurdles.

"When it started to get dark, we had to be in the house before the streetlight stopped flickering," says Gail. "My brother hated that rule. I would be a little mother, tugging him in, explaining to him that later he'd understand. My mom says I've always been old."

Gail didn't mind going home because there she could do something she has always loved to do: read. She still enjoys reading today. "I love long novels," she says. "I have to slow myself down. I'm always whipping through 500 pages in a day and a half. I'm mad when a book is *over*."

At age 10, Gail remembers, she helped a young friend, who could barely read, to become a good reader. Gail worked with this child all summer long and, by September, Gail's friend was reading two grade levels better than she had been in June.

Reading was the preferred form of entertainment in the Devers household. But the children did get to watch *I Love Lucy*, a comedy on television starring Lucille Ball. Gail became a lifelong fan of the show and has collected videotapes of nearly all 179 episodes!

Books and *Lucy* entertained Gail, but running was her passion. She used to race her older brother and the boys in her neighborhood. "I'd beat 'em in my jeans and [high-top basketball] shoes," she says.

Gail began her track career in high school as a distance runner, then switched to the shorter races. She set a national high school record in the 110-meter hurdles.

Gail received an athletic scholarship to attend the University of California at Los Angeles (UCLA).

★

Before Gail started college in 1984, UCLA hired a new track and field coach for its women's team: Bob Kersee. Gail went to watch the Olympic Trials in Los Angeles and tried to figure out which person was Coach Kersee.

"I got [Olympic sprinter] Valerie Briscoe to point him out," Gail remembers. "He was easy to spot because he was screaming at the top of his lungs at Jackie Joyner. I said, 'Uh, oh, maybe I *can* wait to meet him.'"

(Jackie Joyner-Kersee, who married Bob Kersee in 1986, is considered by many to be the greatest female athlete alive today. She won the 1988 and 1992 Olympic gold medals in the heptathlon, an exhausting seven-event track and field competition.)

A few months later, the Olympic Games were held in Los Angeles. Coach Kersee got Gail a ticket to see some of the track and field events. "He told me he wanted me to go in person and watch because, by 1988, I could be an Olympian myself," says Gail. "I thought, 'This man is crazy.'"

Coach Kersee knew talent when he saw it. Gail became a dominant force in college. At a meet during her junior year, she got six first-place finishes, winning the 100 meters, 200 meters, 100-meter hurdles, long jump, and running the anchor, or last, leg on the victorious 4 x 100-meter and 4 x 400-meter relays. In 1988, as a senior, she was the national college champion in the 100 meters and finished third in the 100-meter hurdles.

Gail earned a place on the U.S. Track and Field Team that summer by finishing second in the hurdles at the Olympic Trials. Her coach's prediction had come true. At age 21, Gail Devers was an Olympian.

★

It was at the 1988 Olympic Games in Seoul, South Korea, that Gail first noticed the signs of the illness that would later be diagnosed as Graves' disease. She had entered the Olympics as one of the favorites in the women's 100-meter hurdles, but she ran poorly and didn't even qualify for the final. "Mentally, I was up and ready to run," Gail remembers, "but physically, my body was saying 'Gail, I just can't do it.'"

When she returned to the United States from Seoul her physical condition worsened. She began to get blurred vision and bad headaches. She either slept all day or was unable to sleep a wink. Her hands shook and her hair began to fall out. Her weight fell from 115 pounds to

Cool Fact

Gail loves monkeys and has a large collection of stuffed ones. She also has a curiosity for the gross and unusual. "I ask people to take off bandages so I can look at their sores," she says.

97 pounds and then jumped to 137 pounds. She couldn't remember things, not even her own phone number and address.

"My coach would tell me to do something and I'd walk across the track and forget what he said," Gail says. "The doctors said I was just tired."

The doctors prescribed rest, but it didn't work. Finally, in September 1990, they discovered that Gail had Graves' disease, which is an illness that affects the thyroid gland.

Located in the neck, the thyroid gland controls a person's energy level. Graves' disease makes the thyroid grow abnormally and produce too much of a chemical, called a hormone, that overstimulates the other organs in the body. This can cause such problems as an irregular heartbeat, weight loss, muscle weakness, and nervousness.

"The doctors told me that my disease was two weeks away from becoming cancerous," says Gail. "If it had been cancerous, I would have died within a matter of months. It was scary but it was also a relief. I finally real-

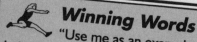

Winning Words

"Use me as an example. If you have faith and believe in yourself, anything is possible because the last three years of my life have been a miracle." — *Gail Devers*

ized that I wasn't going crazy. There was a reason I was feeling bad."

But Gail's problems were only beginning. Doctors wanted to prescribe certain drugs to treat the condition, but Gail did not want to take them because they were on the International Olympic Committee's list of banned substances. Athletes may be banned for life from competition for taking drugs on that list.

Instead, Gail's doctors started her on chemotherapy [KEE-mo-THAIR-ah-pee] and radiation treatments. In chemotherapy, patients are given large doses of strong drugs. In radiation, X rays are used to zap cancer cells. Both treatments were intended to shrink Gail's thyroid and get the hormone levels down to normal.

During the treatments, Gail had even more painful physical problems. "My feet started swelling and bleeding," she recalls. "Every time I tried to take a step, I started crying. I began crawling on my knees, so I wouldn't have to walk. I was carried into the bathroom and out."

Gail was put into the hospital. It turned out her feet had been burned by the radiation. "They said that if I had walked on them for two more days," says Gail, "they would have had to amputate [surgically cut off] my feet."

The possibility of losing her feet was the scariest part of the whole ordeal for Gail. "You take it for granted that you can get up and walk across the room, get up in the morning and walk to the bathroom or car," she says.

"I love track and field so much that I don't know what I would have done had I lost my feet. I now thank God every day that I have them."

Gail stayed in bed for an entire month and slowly her feet healed. In March 1991, she returned to UCLA. "I couldn't run, but Bobby [Coach Kersee] brought a stationary bicycle out to the track and I'd ride it while everybody else was running," she remembers.

As her feet improved, Gail increased her workouts on the stationary bike. By April, she was able to walk around the UCLA track in her socks. Then she began to jog. Soon she was running full speed again.

Her training schedule became more intense. She would work out on the UCLA track for four hours every weekday, then go to the weight room for more work. She reached the point where she could squat lift 300 pounds, earning the nicknames "Mighty Mite" and "Little Hercules" from her teammates.

In May, Gail competed in her first hurdles race since the 1988 Olympics and posted a competitive time. In June, she went to New York City to compete in The Athletics Congress (TAC) national championships. She was entered in the hurdles and many of her competitors were surprised to see her back so soon.

Gail had set a goal of finishing in the top three, but nobody thought she could do it. She qualified for the final, and right before the championship race, Gail and

Coach Kersee walked into a grassy area and prayed. "Lord, you've brought us a long way," said Coach Kersee, who, like Gail's dad, is a Baptist minister. "Please help us get through just 10 more hurdles." Then they both cried. After drying her eyes, Gail went out and won the race!

She contined to improve each week. In August, she finished second in the 100-meter hurdles at the world championships in Tokyo, Japan. "I was the happiest silver medalist in Tokyo," she says.

Eleven days later, Gail won the 100-meter hurdles in a meet in Berlin, Germany. In that race, she set an American record of 12.48 seconds. It had been less than a year since Gail was bedridden with Graves' disease. Gail's comeback was complete. As she put it, "I felt like somebody was watching out for me."

★

Now that Gail had run so well in Japan and Germany, the idea of running in the 1992 Summer Olympics in Barcelona, Spain, did not seem so farfetched. She even went to the United States Olympic Trials and qualified for the U.S. track and field team in not one, but two

Notable Quote
"It takes a while for the bulb to go on in Gail's head, but once it does, and she sees what she's capable of, she's unstoppable." — Bobby Kersee, *Gail's coach*

events — the hurdles and the 100-meter dash.

Gail was not ranked among the top women in the world in the 100 meters, but Coach Kersee had convinced her that she had the skills needed to win the event. Besides great speed, an athlete needs quickness, determination, and concentration to win a short race like the 100-meter dash or hurdles.

Coach Kersee says that arrogance — a feeling that you're the best — is also important to being a good sprinter. "Gail is not naturally aggressive enough," he once explained. "Gail isn't exactly nonchalant, but she doesn't have the innate sprinter's nastiness. That's fine, dealing with her as a person, but not as a sprinter."

How It Works

The 100-meter race is the most famous sprint. It is a race of pure speed. Sprinters explode out of the starting blocks, aim to reach full speed as quickly as possible, then try to hold on until the finish. The winner of the women's race at the Olympics or world championships also wins the title "the world's fastest woman." Florence Griffith Joyner set the women's 100-meter world record of 10.49 seconds in 1988. Hurdlers combine awesome speed with great flexibility and agility. They must run at full speed *and* leap hurdles! There are 10 hurdles in a race and, in women's events, they are 33" high. The world record for women in the 100-meter hurdles is 12.21 seconds, set by Yordanka Donkova of Bulgaria, also in 1988.

Four years earlier, when Gail was a freshman at UCLA, Coach Kersee had believed she would be an Olympic champion by 1992. Now he had to constantly remind her of how good she was and what she was capable of accomplishing.

In Barcelona, Gail was not the favorite in the 100-meter dash. But she won it — in one of the closest women's 100 meters in Olympic history. Gail finished in 10.82 seconds, and the next four runners finished just six-hundreths of a second behind her. The race was so close that officials had to study a photograph taken at the finish line to decide who had won.

"I had no idea who won," Gail said later. "Everyone was looking up at the picture [on the screen by the scoreboard]. I still couldn't tell who won. I didn't know I'd won until the man announced it on the loudspeaker."

Gail, the underdog, had won a gold medal. She would be the favorite in the 100-meter hurdles, her better event, five days later. Could she win another gold?

It didn't happen. Gail was leading the race as she approached the last hurdle. But her lead leg caught the top of the hurdle, and she tripped and fell! She managed to scramble across the finish line, but came in only a distant fifth.

To most people, it would be heartbreaking to come so close to a second Olympic gold medal and fall just short. But Gail took the defeat in stride. After all, she had accomplished so much just by making it to the Olympics!

Of her failure to win the 100 meters, Gail would only say,
"It just wasn't meant to be."

★

After her gold medal victory in Barcelona, Gail turned her
focus on the future, and what she might like to do next.
One of her goals is to become involved in education and
to work with kids.

The city of San Diego, Gail's hometown, made her
an "Ambassador of Education." She now speaks to elementary school kids in the city to stress the importance
of learning.

When she is finished with track — and she does
not know when that will be — Gail would like to open a
children's day-care center. She would also like to create
books and music that will help children learn. Gail has
already written songs for kids. "I taught my goddaughter
Shawnquintavia to spell her name with a song," she says.
That couldn't have been easy!

But Gail's children's projects are still very much for
the future. There's still too much running to do! At the
1993 World Outdoor Track and Field Championships in
Stuttgart, Germany, Gail won the 100-meter dash in a
photo finish, and she has her eye on the 1996 Summer
Olympics in Atlanta, Georgia. Often, Gail trains with her
close friend Jackie Joyner-Kersee.

Gail still must take a little yellow pill every day, as
a result of her thyroid condition. Her thyroid was
destroyed by the treatment, and the medicine replaces the

DAVE BLACK

The ice is Oksana Baiul's stage. Her grace, athleticism, and personality made her an Olympic figure skating champion by age 16.

Although small in size, Gail Devers has powered herself to world championships in both sprinting and hurdling.

MIKE POWELL/ALLSPORT

A blur (here in pink) on the track, Julie Krone has the strength and smarts to guide half-ton horses to victory.

Steffi Graf's skill and determination have made her a tennis legend at age 25. She once won five straight Grand Slam events and 66 consecutive matches!

DAVE BLACK

A skater almost since she could walk, Bonnie Blair won gold medals in speed skating at three different Olympic Games.

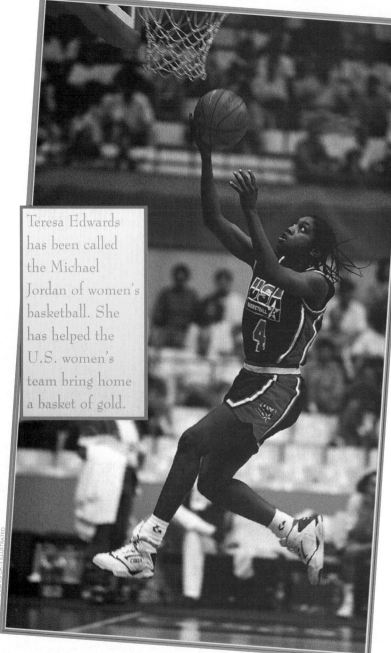

Teresa Edwards has been called the Michael Jordan of women's basketball. She has helped the U.S. women's team bring home a basket of gold.

Nancy Lopez is a great come-from-behind player. Her exciting style electrified women's golf and earned her a place in the Hall of Fame by age 30.

Shannon Miller is a quiet young woman with explosive talent. The gymnast burst out of Oklahoma to win five Olympic medals and back-to-back world titles.

DAVE BLACK

missing hormones that a healthy thyroid would produce. She will have to take the medicine for the rest of her life. "It's a small price to pay for still being here," she says.

As you might expect, Gail doesn't let many of life's pitfalls get her down. She's already been through so much.

Says Gail: "I don't feel there's any hurdle too high or any obstacle in my life that I can't get over." ★

TRAILBLAZER: WILMA RUDOLPH

Like Gail Devers, Wilma Rudolph had to overcome physical challenges to succeed as a sprinter. Wilma was born prematurely and weighed only 4 ½ pounds at birth. She suffered through polio, double pneumonia, and scarlet fever, which left her with a crippled left leg. She wore a steel brace on her leg and needed painful massages. Eventually, she was able to replace the brace with an orthopedic shoe. Then one day, when Wilma was 12, her mother came home to find her playing basketball barefoot! Wilma went on to become a star athlete and won three gold medals at the 1960 Summer Olympics in the 100- and 200-meter sprints and in the 4 x 100-meter relay.

Julie Krone

When Julie Krone was a kid, she had a dream. She wanted to become a jockey.

It was a tough dream to follow. A woman trying to break into horse racing had to face down many doubters. There were few women jockeys in the sport and even fewer who could consistently win races!

Trainers told Julie it was a sport for men, not girls. Jockeys must have strong hands and legs to guide a horse that can weigh more than 1,200 pounds. They thought the 4' 10 ½", 100-pound Julie was not strong enough.

But Julie remained true to her dream. By the time she was 25 years old, she had become not only the best female jockey in history, but one of the best jockeys in the world.

Few have been born to horse racing the way Julie was. Her mother, Judi,

JULIE KRONE
Born: July 24, 1963
Birthplace: Benton Harbor, Michigan
Height: 4' 10 ½"
Weight: 100 pounds

Julie's toughness and skill at handling 1,200-pound racehorses have won her many riding titles and a place as one of the top jockeys today.

was an award-winning equestrian (horse-show) rider.
Julie's father, Don, was an art and photography teacher at
Lake Michigan College, and the family lived on a horse
farm in Eau Claire, Michigan.

Julie was only 2 years old when her mother put her
on a horse for the first time. Her mother was trying to sell
a horse to another woman and put Julie, still in diapers,
aboard to prove how gentle the horse was. The horse
walked off and stopped at a wall. Julie reached down,
grabbed the reins and tugged them to one side. The horse
turned and trotted back. Julie was a born rider.

From that moment, all Julie wanted to do was ride
horses. She started on a pony and learned to be a trick
rider. Trick riders perform in circuses and rodeos, doing
stunts while the horse gallops at full speed. Julie could
stand up on a horse and ride it by the time she was 13.

Julie's mother taught her the finer points of being
an equestrian rider, such as how to hold her hands and
arch her back properly so that the horse would take direc-
tion better. When Julie was only 5, she won an equestri-

Winning Ways

Julie was the first woman ever to win a riding
title at a major track. She is one of three U.S. jockeys
ever to win six races in one day at a track, and the first
female jockey to win a Triple Crown race. She has won
more than 1,200 races.

an blue ribbon in a 21-and-under fair competition!

Julie entered and won many horse shows as a youngster, but she never let go of her dream of being a jockey. She read about horses, and wrote poems and painted pictures of them. She watched on television as jockey Steve Cauthen, then 18, won horse racing's biggest prize, the Triple Crown, aboard Affirmed in 1978, and she developed a schoolgirl's crush on the jockey. (To win the Triple Crown, a horse must win the Kentucky Derby, Preakness Stakes, and Belmont Stakes races.)

Julie once described her love of horses this way: "Shakespeare says, 'There's no secret so close as between a horse and a rider,' and it's true. You just look in their eyes. The horses with a lot of talent always seem like they're looking into the way beyond. They always have the look of eagles in their eyes. It's very romantic."

When Julie mentioned her ambition to her class-mates, they laughed. Sometimes that made her so angry she started throwing punches.

Few people took Julie seriously. She may have been a teenager, but she looked as if she were in grade school. She weighed only 90 pounds and wasn't even 5' tall. Sure, jockeys were small but they weren't this small!

At 15, Julie nearly joined a circus as a trick rider, but she backed out at the last minute. Then her parents got divorced. Julie's older brother (by three years), Donnie, went to live with Mr. Krone, while Julie stayed with her mom. Julie felt more alone than ever.

During spring vacation in 1979, when she was almost 16, Julie and her mother visited Churchill Downs, the famous racetrack in Louisville, Kentucky, which is the site of the Kentucky Derby. There, they met trainer Clarence Picou. Clarence agreed to give Julie a summer job walking and grooming horses. *(For an explanation of racing jobs, see How It Works, page 43.)*

Julie lived with Clarence and his wife, Donna. Every day, Julie went to the track to ride and care for the horses. After three months, she returned to Michigan. But her determination to become a jockey was as strong as ever.

Finally, in the middle of her senior year of high school, Julie couldn't wait any longer. She dropped out of school and flew to Tampa, Florida. She had decided that she would live with her grandparents and use Tampa Bay Downs racetrack to get her start as a jockey.

It wasn't so easy. When Julie showed up at the track gate, the guard did not believe that this little girl was there to look for a job as a jockey and wouldn't let her in.

Julie climbed over the fence. A woman driving through the grounds stopped. She thought she had found a little lost girl. But when the woman heard Julie's story, she took her to see trainer Jerry Pace.

Jerry gave Julie a chance to show her stuff on a training track, and she impressed him enough to be given a mount, or horse to ride, in a race. Five weeks later, in February 1980, Julie had her first winner! In her first 48 rides, she had nine winners, four seconds, and 10 thirds.

Julie Snellings, a former jockey who was working in the Tampa Bay Downs office, persuaded her former agent, Chick Lang, to get Julie some mounts at tracks in the northeast. Chick managed to get Julie some rides, but she often ran into resistance from horsemen.

"Nobody took girl riders seriously — they were a joke," recalls trainer John Forbes. "Nobody thought a girl was strong enough. The jockeys didn't ride harder against them; if anything they rode a little easier, because nobody wanted to be the one to get a girl hurt, and nobody worried that a girl might beat him. It ate Julie up to be considered a 'girl jockey.' I introduced her to someone as a 'jockette.' She kicked me in the shins."

Julie tried to convince everyone how tough she was. She wouldn't wear makeup, jewelry, or any clothes that made her look like a girl. She even started to walk and talk like a boy. When shaking hands with horse owners and trainers, she would squeeze their hands really hard. She even got into fistfights with grooms!

Cool Fact

Julie still does trick and equestrian riding, and does it well. She has competed in celebrity equestrian events. Many veteran riders believe Julie could compete on the equestrian circuit if she wanted to.

Julie was determined. She moved from track to track, sometimes riding five races in the afternoon at one track, and then riding five more at night at another track. She wanted to be noticed so she would get better mounts.

Eventually that happened. Julie rode well and she got better horses to ride. Trainers said she had "magic hands." She reminded them, they said, of the great Bill Shoemaker, who rode for 41 years and holds the all-time record of 8,833 races won.

"Julie is an extremely patient rider," says jockey Richard Migliore. "She just sits there with a long hold [loose rein], not moving much, and the horses respond. I am an agressive rider. I pick up the horse's head and hold the reins taut. I make the demand. Julie does not demand. She asks the question and gets the result."

In 1982, at age 19, Julie won more races than any other jockey during the racing season at Atlantic City (New Jersey) Race Course to win the riding title. But that didn't make things much easier.

Some of the male jockeys were jealous of Julie's success and tried to intimidate her. One jockey smacked

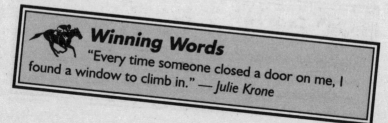

Winning Words
"Every time someone closed a door on me, I found a window to climb in." — *Julie Krone*

her horse across the head with his whip. He said it was an accident, but Julie didn't buy it. She pushed him off the weigh-in scales before another race. When another jockey slashed her ear with his whip at Monmouth Park in New Jersey, she punched him in the face. When he tackled her into the jockey's swimming pool, she hit him with a lounge chair.

Through it all Julie kept winning races. That gained her the respect of the other jockeys and, more importantly, trainers. She won the Atlantic City riding title again in 1983.

★

In the fall of 1983, Julie suffered her first major injury. She fell off a mount during a workout at Laurel Racetrack in Maryland. She broke her back and couldn't ride for four months.

When she returned to action, Julie fell into a slump for the first time in her career. She did not win a race in 80 starts and got very discouraged.

Things got worse. One day in 1986, Julie got a phone call from her mother. Her mother had just found out that she had cancer and had only a short time to live.

Julie was crushed. "I remember I was sitting in my room, crying and thinking all the things you think about at a time like that: how unfair it is, all the things I should have done for her, how much I loved her," Julie recalls.

"I didn't know what to say to my mom. You feel so helpless at a time like that. There's not really anything you can say except that you'll be there for them. "

At first, Julie couldn't concentrate on her races because she was so worried about her mother. She did terribly that day. She was left in the starting gate in one race, fell off her mount after another race, and dropped her whip in a third.

This went on for several months. Julie had always phoned her mother regularly, and her mother noticed that Julie wasn't confiding in her the way she once had. Julie admitted that she was so worried about her mother, her own problems seemed small.

Julie's mother told her that she wanted to hear about everything that was happening — the good days and bad ones, too. So Julie began telling her all about the trouble she was having at the track. One day, while Julie's mother was taking treatments at the hospital, she said to Julie, "Come on, win one for me today, okay?"

Later that day as Julie was driving to work, she said to herself, "That's it! That's what I'm going to do. I'm going to go out and win some races for Mom."

Julie won three races that day and started winning regularly. In 1987, she was the leading rider at both Monmouth and the Meadowlands, another New Jersey track. "I decided to be positive for my mother's sake, instead of being negative because of my concern for her," Julie said.

As Julie continued to win, a wonderful thing happened. Her mother began to get better. A year after she was supposed to die, Mrs. Krone not only was still alive, she felt well enough to return to training horses.

Julie continued to climb in the world of horse racing. In 1988, she became the first woman to ride in the Breeders' Cup, one of racing's biggest events, and she beat Bill Shoemaker in a match race (a race between two horses) at Arlington Park in Chicago, Illinois. She set a record by winning six races in one day at the Meadowlands in 1989, and won riding titles there and at Monmouth in 1988 and 1989.

Most important to Julie, the other jockeys began treating her as one of them. She was no longer a "girl jockey." She was simply a winner.

Julie missed much of the 1990 season after a riding accident left her with a badly fractured left arm. But she returned to win her very first race back, at Monmouth Park in July. She kept on winning, and in 1992 and 1993 led all jockeys in victories at Florida's Gulfstream Park.

In the spring of 1993, Julie set out to do something no

How It Works

Trainers are like coaches for racehorses. They are responsible for getting the horse ready and deciding which rider and strategy to use in a race. A groom is responsible for the cleaning and feeding of the horses.

female jockey had ever done before: win a Triple Crown race. Her big chance came at the Belmont Stakes at New York City's Belmont Park in June.

Julie was given the mount aboard a horse named Colonial Affair. The race was close, and the horses were bunched at the top of the home stretch when Julie and Colonial Affair suddenly charged into the lead. Colonial Affair outran the other horses to the finish line and carried Julie into the history books.

Julie's good fortune continued in August at Saratoga Racecourse in Saratoga Springs, New York. On August 20, she won five races, becoming only the third jockey ever to win five races in one day at Saratoga.

But on August 30, the final day of the season at the

TRAILBLAZER: ROBYN SMITH

Before Julie came along, the best female jockey of all time was Robyn Smith. Robyn grew up in San Francisco, California. Like Julie, she was turned down for mounts time after time, but she eventually proved herself at New York's tough tracks: Aqueduct, Belmont, and Saratoga. Robyn became one of the leading New York jockeys in 1972, and in March 1973, she became the first female jockey to win a major stakes race. After she left racing, Robyn married the famous dancer and movie star Fred Astaire.

track, Julie was involved in a racing accident that could have killed her. Coming off the final turn in the third race, a horse moved into the path of Julie's mount. The two horses bumped and Julie's horse crashed headfirst into the turf, sending Julie head-over-heels through the air. She landed hard on her right ankle, facing one of the oncoming horses. Julie caught a flying hoof right in her chest that knocked her into a backward somersault.

She remembered being afraid for her life. "Pow!" she said. "I got hit on the heart. My arm was cut so you could see the elbow socket. My ankle hurt so bad I kept thinking, 'Pass out. Please, pass out.' But I didn't. I was really scared."

Fortunately for Julie, she was wearing a protective vest. If she hadn't been wearing one, the doctors said, she might have been killed. The bones in her right ankle were shattered and one elbow was knocked out of its socket.

Julie was rushed to Saratoga Hospital and had surgery on her ankle. Then she was taken to a hospital in New York City and underwent two more operations. Julie remained in the hospital for just three weeks but it took her nine months before she was able to ride a horse again.

She finally got the okay to race again in the spring of 1994. On May 25, 1994, Julie finished third in her first race. The next day, she won aboard a dark bay filly named Consider the Lily.

The little girl with the heart as big as her dreams stood tall in the saddle once again. ★

Steffi Graf

When Steffi Graf was 3 years old, she was fascinated by the tennis rackets her father kept in the closet. She would bring them to him and ask him to teach her to play.

At first, Peter Graf would protest. He was too tired. He did not have the time or patience.

But Steffi would not give up. Finally, Mr. Graf surrendered. He sawed off the end of an old racket, gave Steffi a few tips, and let her bat balls against the living room walls. Steffi made her own court in the basement by running a string between two chairs. Mr. Graf played matches with her there, offering prizes of ice cream.

Steffi is still playing and still winning prizes. The little girl who loved tennis grew up to become one of the greatest tennis players of all time.

★

Steffi's talent for tennis changed her life. She won

STEFFI GRAF

Born: June 14, 1969
Birthplace: Brühl, Germany
Height: 5' 9"
Weight: 132 pounds

Steffi is only the third woman ever to win the Grand Slam of tennis, capturing the sport's four biggest tournaments in the same year.

her first junior tournament when she was 6 years old. When Steffi was 7, Mr. Graf decided to become her coach. Mr. Graf was an excellent recreational player and was the Number 1 player at his tennis club.

When Steffi was 8, her father gave up his businesses, which included an automobile dealership and an insurance agency, to devote himself to tennis full time. He and his wife, Heidi, built the Graf Tennis Club, with three outdoor and three indoor courts, in their hometown of Brühl, West Germany (now Germany).

Mr. Graf was a good coach, and Steffi got better and better as a player. At 13, she won the German Junior Championship in the 18- and-under division.

Steffi had an outstanding slicing backhand stroke that few players her age could handle. She was also beginning to develop a powerful forehand to go with it. She dominated the junior division so completely that amateur tennis was no longer a challenge for her.

So, that same year, Steffi became a professional tennis player. Within weeks, she received a world ranking — Number 214. She was the second youngest player

Winning Ways

Steffi has won Wimbledon five times, the U.S. Open three times, the Australian Open three times, and the French Open three times. She won all four Grand Slam events plus the Olympic gold medal in 1988.

ever to be ranked internationally *(see How It Works, page 56)*.

Steffi quit school in the eighth grade, and her father hired a tutor to travel with them on the pro tour. The tutor instructed Steffi until she was 15. After that, Steffi continued her education by mail. She received assignments from a teacher through the mail, completed the work, and sent it back.

It didn't take Steffi long to show that she could play with the best in the world. In the summer of 1984, when she was 15, Steffi reached the quarterfinals at Wimbledon, England's prestigious tournament. She also won the women's championship at the 1984 Summer Olympic Games in Los Angeles, California, where tennis was a demonstration sport. (A demonstration sport is not contested for medals, but to demonstrate, or show, the sport.) With her strong performances, Steffi jumped to Number 22 on the computer rankings list!

Steffi continued to climb up the rankings in 1985. She reached the round of 16 at the important French Open and Wimbledon tournaments. At the U.S. Open in Flushing Meadow, New York, she advanced to the quarterfinals, where she faced Pam Shriver.

Her match with Pam was a classic. All three sets ended in a 6–6 draw and a tiebreaker had to be used each time to determine the winner. Steffi won the first set, but Pam came back to win the second. Pam was ahead, 5–3, in the third set, but Steffi came back to tie it, 6–6. Then Steffi won the set and the match in a tiebreaker.

The match took 2 hours and 45 minutes to complete and was the first match in modern women's tennis ever to go 39 games, the maximum allowed under tennis rules. When it was over, Pam broke down in tears on the sidelines. "It was unbelievable," she said. "I couldn't have put in more effort, and it was two points too few."

Although Steffi would lose to Martina Navratilova in the semifinals, many tennis observers said that her match with Pam was one of the best of the season.

★

After the U.S. Open, Steffi's father insisted that she take some time off. Every year, in fact, he makes Steffi take six weeks of vacation from competitive tennis. "I have to be careful with Steffi," Mr. Graf once explained. "Steffi works much harder than the other girls because she wants to. I have never pushed her. That is why she is so good."

Steffi confirmed what her dad said. "It's tough keeping my hands off a racket," she said.

Although Steffi looked like a typical teenager — wearing T-shirts, jeans, and loafers most of the time — she did not share in many of the life experiences of her friends. Tennis always came before any social activities. She didn't date and she had few close friends. She did not make friends easily with other players for fear of losing her competitive edge.

Once during a week-long exhibition in Mexico,

Steffi avoided sitting by the pool or playing volleyball with the other tennis players. Instead, she stayed in her room with her mother, even eating her meals there.

"You're not really friends with anyone on the tour because everyone's thinking of herself," Steffi once explained. "Everyone wants to win."

Steffi also avoided most of the parties on the tour, preferring to stay in her hotel room and play cards with her father, read (she enjoys Ernest Hemingway and Stephen King novels), or listen to music (she likes rock). She felt partying wore down the other players.

Steffi's self-discipline is legendary. She has a strict training routine, designed by her father, that includes running, weight lifting, and jumping rope with weights on her ankles. She also spends several hours a day on the tennis court, playing Pavel Slozil, her hitting instructor.

But it takes more than dedication to make a great player. Steffi has great physical size and strength. Long legged and slim, Steffi is 5' 9" tall, weighs 132 pounds, and has unusually long arms and big hands. One of her

Cool Fact

Like many famous people, Steffi does not like to be photographed. But she loves taking photographs and brings her camera with her whenever she's traveling. She says her favorite place to take photographs is New York City because it's so crowded that no one notices her.

greatest strengths is her powerful topspin forehand, which is considered by many experts to be the best in the history of women's tennis. Steffi also has a devastating serve and great speed, which enables her to cover the court better than any other woman in the game today.

★

Steffi's goal was to become the Number 1 player in the world, and she continued to climb the world rankings. In April of 1986, she won her first major tournament, defeating Chris Evert in the final of the Family Circle Magazine Cup in Hilton Head, South Carolina. Defeating a tennis legend like Chris gave Steffi a lot of confidence. She won seven more tournaments during the year.

In 1987, Steffi emerged as a star. Going into the French Open, she had won six tournaments in a row. The French Open is played on clay. Clay is different from other court surfaces, such as grass or hard court, because it slows down the bounce of the ball. Steffi's game is suited well to clay because she is a "baseliner." She attacks from the back of the court with well-placed shots.

Steffi reached the final of the French Open, where

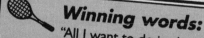

Winning words:
"All I want to do is play good tennis and have fun. I want so much to hit it hard — and have it go in."
— *Steffi Graf*

she met Martina Navratilova. Martina was the top player in the game and had held the year-end Number 1 ranking for five straight years. But Steffi had beaten Martina in a match in February and was confident she could do so again.

Martina had yet to win a tournament in 1987. On top of that, she did not particularly like to play on clay. Martina was a "serve-and-volley" player. That means she liked to rush the net and hit fast shots beyond the reach of her opponent. The clay surface slowed down her shots, which allowed opponents to return them.

The two players battled evenly through the first two sets. Steffi won the first, 6–4, and Martina took the second by the same score. Steffi was leading in the decisive third set, 7–6, but Martina was serving and in a position to tie it up. Instead, Martina committed a double-fault, twice hitting the ball into the net on her serve, to hand Steffi the match.

Steffi was happy for the victory but sorry it had come that way. "If she had not double-faulted, I don't think I would have won," she said.

One month later, Steffi met Martina again — in the final of Wimbledon. Martina, whose game was better suited to the fast grass courts of Wimbledon's All-England Lawn Tennis and Croquet Club, won 7–5, 6–3. It was her sixth Wimbledon singles title in a row, a record.

Six weeks later, Steffi defeated Chris Evert, 6–3, 6–4 at the Virginia Slims Tournament in Los Angeles.

When the computer printed out its rankings, Steffi became the Number 1 player in women's tennis.

Steffi was thrilled. "I can't stop smiling," she said.

But Martina was not smiling. Although she had won only the Wimbledon title during the year, she believed the Number 1 position still belonged to her. She vowed to beat Steffi at the upcoming U.S. Open and reclaim the Number 1 ranking.

Sure enough, Steffi and Martina met in the final at Flushing Meadow. However, Steffi was weak from having battled the flu all week. Martina won, 7-6, 6-1.

Martina insisted that she should be ranked Number 1, but the computer still gave Steffi the honor because she had already won seven tournaments in 1987, including the important French Open. Steffi knew, though, that she would have to win one more tournament to be Number 1 at the end of the year.

The final tournament of the year was the Virginia Slims Championship at New York's Madison Square Garden in November. Only the top 16 ranked players in the world are invited to participate in this tournament.

Once again, Steffi reached the final. This time, her opponent was Gabriela Sabatini. In most women's match-es, the first player to win two sets wins the match. In the Virginia Slims, though, a player has to win three sets. Gabriela won the first set, but Steffi rallied to win the next three and earn the title.

Steffi had won an incredible 11 tournaments in

1987 to stake her claim as the best in the game. Her record in matches for the year was 75–2. Surely she couldn't do any better. But believe it or not, 1988 turned out to be her greatest year.

There are four tournaments that are considered the biggest events on the tennis calendar each year. They are the Australian Open, the French Open, Wimbledon, and the U.S. Open. They are known as the Grand Slam tournaments. Only once every few decades has a player won all four in one year. That accomplishment is known as winning the Grand Slam.

In 1988, Steffi Graf was ready to take her game to a higher level. She began the year, in January, by winning the Australian Open, defeating Chris Evert in the final. In May, she went to Paris, France, to play in the French Open, and whipped 17-year-old Natalia Zvereva, 6–0, 6–0, in a match that lasted only 32 minutes!

The next major event on the schedule was Wimbledon, and Steffi knew it would probably mean a

Notable Quote

"I like Steffi's sporting attitude, shyness, and family image. She is good for the game. We need young people like her at the top so that the younger players can look up to them." — *Margaret Smith Court, who won the Grand Slam in 1970*

rematch with Martina Navratilova, who had defeated her the year before in the finals of both Wimbledon and the U.S. Open. Steffi took some time off and, since Martina is left-handed, practiced against a left-handed male player. The man hit balls repeatedly to Steffi's backhand, which is considered the weakest part of her game.

The strategy worked well. At Wimbledon, Steffi easily beat her opponents leading up to the final. As expected, Martina was there, waiting for her.

Steffi was nervous in the beginning of the match and lost the first set, 5–7. She even trailed in the second set, 0–2. But Steffi came roaring back. She rallied to win the set, 6–2, then completely dominated the third set, 6–1. Steffi won 12 of the last 13 games in the match, repeatedly scoring with a crosscourt backhand and down-the-line returns of Martina's serve.

Martina was gracious in defeat. "This is how it should happen," she said. "I lost to a better player on the

How It Works

The Women's Tennis Association determines a player's ranking with a points system. During a tournament, a player is awarded points for each round she wins. She also receives bonus points for beating a highly ranked player. Players are awarded the most points for winning Grand Slam tournaments. The players accumulate points and are ranked according to how many points they have.

final day. This is the end of a chapter, passing the torch."

The spotlight was now clearly on Steffi to complete the Grand Slam with a win in the U.S. Open. Playing under extreme pressure in New York, she breezed through the early rounds, but another formidable opponent, Gabriela Sabatini, was waiting in the final. Like Martina, Gabriela had given Steffi plenty of trouble in the past. This meeting was no exception.

Steffi won the first set, 6–3, but she seemed very nervous during the second set. She committed several errors and Gabriela won the set, 6–3, to set up a decisive third set. But Gabriela had already given everything she had and had no endurance left for the third set. Steffi overpowered her, and moved out to a commanding 5–1 lead. She needed to win just one more game for the title.

As soon as her backhand shot whizzed down the line to win the game, set, and match, Steffi threw her racket into the air and raced into the stands to hug her family. Steffi had completed a Grand Slam sweep! Only Margaret Smith Court and Maureen Connolly, among women players, had ever achieved such a feat!

Just a few days later, Steffi was in Seoul, South Korea, to represent West Germany in the Olympics. By that time, tennis was an official medal sport, and Steffi capped her brilliant year by beating Gabriela again in the final to win the gold medal.

Steffi's winning streak continued until Pam Shriver halted it at 46 consecutive matches in the semifinals of the Virginia Slims Masters tournament in November 1988. In January 1989, though, Steffi bounced back to win the Australian Open, her fifth consecutive victory in a Grand Slam tournament!

The Grand Slam streak was stopped when Steffi lost to Arantxa Sanchez Vicario in the final of the 1989 French Open. But on June 26, 1989, Steffi launched another winning streak. This one lasted 66 matches before it ended on May 20, 1990. It was the second longest winning streak in modern history and included three more Grand Slam crowns — the 1989 Wimbledon and U.S. Open titles, and the 1990 Australian Open championship.

Steffi's dominance was overwhelming. She was the Number 1 player for 186 straight weeks, from August 17, 1987 to March 10, 1991 — longer than anyone in the history of tennis. In 1991, she won the first of three straight Wimbledon crowns, and in 1993, she came within an eyelash of completing another Grand Slam sweep. She won the French, Wimbledon, and U.S. Open titles that year, but lost in the final of the Australian Open.

Steffi was displaced as the best player in the world for a while by Monica Seles, the Yugoslavian-born, U.S.-trained star. Still, Steffi persevered. Physical problems (and an attack by a crazed fan) forced Monica off the tour, and soon Steffi was back on top.

Steffi has been on the tour for 11 years and has

earned many millions of dollars through her victories and endorsements. But she shows no signs of slowing down. She won 10 tournaments in 1993 and continued to play a full schedule in 1994.

She also shows few signs of being such a wealthy sports star. Steffi once refused to buy a handbag for $33 because she felt it was too expensive. Another time, she was in Chicago in the winter and did not have an overcoat to keep warm. Her father had to tell her to buy a coat because she did not want to spend $230 on it.

It shouldn't be surprising that money means very little to Steffi. She has really been interested in only one thing since she was 3 years old: hitting a tennis ball better than anyone else. ★

TRAILBLAZER: MAUREEN CONNOLLY

Maureen Connolly was the first female player ever to win all four Grand Slam events in the same year. She accomplished the feat in 1953. Nicknamed "Little Mo," she dominated women's tennis from 1952–54. After winning the Grand Slam in 1953, she seemed ready to repeat her victory in 1954 after winning the French Open and Wimbledon. But a horseback-riding accident prevented her from competing in the U.S. or Australian Opens. The accident severely damaged her leg and forced her to retire.

Bonnie Blair

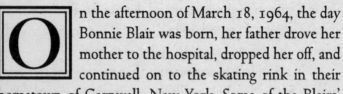

On the afternoon of March 18, 1964, the day Bonnie Blair was born, her father drove her mother to the hospital, dropped her off, and continued on to the skating rink in their hometown of Cornwall, New York. Some of the Blairs' other children were competing in a speed skating meet and Mr. Blair was the official timekeeper.

"He knew he was going to have to wait [for the baby to be born]," Bonnie once explained. "He figured it might as well be at the rink." That's where Bonnie's dad learned that his wife had given birth to their sixth child. During the meet, the public-address announcer called out, "Looks like the Blairs have another skater."

Did they ever!

BONNIE BLAIR

Born: March 18, 1964
Birthplace: Cornwall, New York
Height: 5' 5"
Weight: 130 pounds

The Blairs were known as a speed skating family long before Bonnie was born. Bonnie's parents, Charlie and Eleanor, had both

Speed skater Bonnie Blair, here celebrating at the 1994 Winter Olympics, has won more gold medals than any other U.S. female Olympian.

enjoyed ice skating as youngsters. One Christmas before Bonnie was born, they gave three of their children figure skates as gifts. All of the Blair children — sisters Mary, Suzy, and Angela and brothers Chuck and Rob — soon became interested in skating, especially skating fast.

One day, a coach saw the kids skating at the rink and suggested they try competitive speed skating. Soon, the whole family was driving to regional meets on weekends. Four of the Blair kids — not counting Bonnie — went on to win national speed skating titles!

The Blairs participated in a style of speed skating called short-track, or pack-style. Short-track skating became an Olympic event in 1992. It's very different from long-track speed skating (see How It Works, page 64), which has been an Olympic sport for as long as there has been a Winter Olympics — since 1924.

When Bonnie was just a toddler, her brothers and sisters brought her to the rink. She loved ice skating right away. "Bonnie could barely walk, and my older kids would put skates on over her shoes," Bonnie's mother recalls. "They would carry Bonnie around the rink. But Bonnie always wanted to skate by herself. She loved it."

"I can't even remember learning how to skate," says Bonnie. "It comes almost as naturally to me as walking."

When Bonnie was 2 years old, the Blairs moved to Champaign [SHAM-pain], Illinois, where Bonnie's father took a job as a sales manager for a concrete company. The main campus of the University of Illinois is in Champaign, and the city is well known as a center for speed skating. It has wonderful facilities, coaching, and competition. It proved to be the perfect place for Bonnie to develop her speed skating skills.

At age 4, Bonnie entered her first speed skating competiton — in short-track skating. She won some pre-liminary heats in her age division, but her parents and coaches didn't push her. "I was still young enough to be taking naps," Bonnie says. "My mom hated to wake me up. I slept through some of my first races."

By the time she was 6, Bonnie was winning races against skaters three and four years older. At age 7, she competed at the Illinois state championships! Bonnie set her sights on competing in the Olympics one day.

In 1978, when Bonnie was 14, a former Olympic silver medalist from Canada named Cathy Priestner Faminow moved to Champaign to coach speed skating. Coach Faminow began working with Bonnie. Bonnie needed to learn long-track skating if she was going to try

Winning Ways
Bonnie won a gold medal in the 500 meters and a bronze in the 1,000 meters at 1988 Olympics. She won gold medals in the 500 and the 1,000 at the 1992 Olympics, and again in 1994.

for the Olympics. Coach Faminow worked with her on improving her technique, and got Bonnie permission to use the University of Illinois rink for early-morning practice sessions.

"Cathy was around at exactly the right time in my life," Bonnie recalls. "She had a big effect on me. She got me to work on my skating all year round instead of just during the winter months."

In the winter of 1978–79, Bonnie competed in her first long-track races. Her times were good enough to earn her a trip to the Olympic Trials at age 15. Bonnie missed making the U.S. team that competed at the 1980 Winter Olympics in Lake Placid, New York. But she was thrilled at having been invited to compete.

★

Back in Champaign, Bonnie was an all-around athlete at Centennial High School. Besides speed skating, she competed in gymnastics and track.

 How It Works

In short-track, or pack, skating, a group of four to six skaters race each other around a 110-meter track set up in a rink the size of an ice hockey rink. The first person to finish wins. In long-track racing, two skaters compete at the same time on a 400-meter oval. They race against the clock. The racer with the fastest time after all the skaters have competed is the winner.

In 1982, Bonnie's coach told her that if she hoped to make the 1984 Olympic team, she should go to Europe to compete in the World Cup season. The World Cup is a season-long series of competitions in the winter sports. Athletes such as skiers and skaters compete in races in Europe and the United States for points. The athlete with the most points in his or her sport at the end of the season is the World Cup champion of that sport.

Coach Faminow knew that Bonnie needed to face tougher competition. There just weren't enough top competitors in the United States, and, at the time, there were only two refrigerated 400-meter speed skating tracks in the United States. Speed skating is a popular sport in many European countries and there are many more Olympic-sized rinks on which to train.

Bonnie was eager to go to Europe, but she did not have enough money to pay for the trip. Her parents could not help her because her father had just retired from his job. The U.S. Speed Skating Federation told her they did not have funds to sponsor athletes competing abroad.

Bonnie tried to raise the money by herself! She asked several Champaign businessmen to sponsor her, but was turned down. With time running out, she turned to a police officer named Gerry Schweigert, who is the father of one of her high school classmates. He got the police department to conduct a series of bake sales and raffles on Bonnie's behalf. "We immediately wanted to help," recalls Sergeant Danny Strand. "Kids think the police don't care. But we do."

The police department's effort and a surprise contribution from pro basketball player Jack Sikma, who had gone to college with Rob Blair, did the trick. Bonnie raised the $7,000 she needed for her trip.

Bonnie was only 17 when she went to Europe. But she didn't forget about school. She took correspondence courses so she could earn her high school diploma.

★

Bonnie's trip to Europe was a huge success. She improved her times so much that she made the U.S. Olympic team for the 1984 Winter Games. The Olympics were held in the city of Sarajevo, in what was then Yugoslavia. Bonnie competed in the 500-meter event and finished eighth. She was just 19 years old. "I was in total awe the whole time," she later said.

Now Bonnie was determined to return to the Olympics in 1988, and win a medal. This time, money for her training was not as hard to come by. The 1984

 Cool Fact

To boost her energy level before a big race Bonnie often will have a peanut-butter-and-jelly sandwich. After she won two gold medals at the 1994 Lillehammer Olympics, Bonnie was signed to do a peanut butter commercial for television.

Summer Olympics in Los Angeles, California, had made a lot of money, and much of it was given to national sports organizations. The U.S. Speed Skating Federation was able to help pay training expenses for skaters like Bonnie. The Champaign police department also continued to raise money for her. They sold bumper stickers and T-shirts that read: "Champaign Policemen's Favorite Speeder: Olympian Bonnie Blair."

Bonnie knew she would have to improve to win a medal at the 1988 Winter Games. In 1985, she began working with Mike Crowe. Mike was the coach of the national speed skating team and was in charge of a training facility in Butte, Montana. Bonnie spent much of her time training there.

Her training schedule was loaded. It included long workouts on the ice in the morning, then weight training, running, biking, and roller skating in the afternoon.

Bonnie also continued to participate in pack skating. Pack skaters have to be able to start quickly in order to avoid collisions, and Bonnie thought the experience would help improve her long-track starts. But Bonnie wasn't just practicing. She won the world championship in short-track skating in 1986!

All of Bonnie's hard work paid off at the 1986 World Sprint Championships. The World Sprint Championships are long-track championship races in the shorter distances, such as the 500 and 1,000 meters. Bonnie tied for second place in the 500 meters with Christa

Rothenburger of West Germany, the 1984 Olympic gold medalist in that event!

Bonnie then went off to Europe to compete in as many meets as she could. During a 100-day period from 1986 to 1987, she competed in eight different countries and broke the world record for the 500 meters. (Her time was 39.43 seconds.) She also won the World Cup title.

At a World Cup event in Calgary, Alberta, Canada, in December 1987 — only two months before the 1988 Winter Olympics — Christa Rothenburger defeated Bonnie in the 500 meters, setting a world record of 39.39 seconds in the process. However, Bonnie refused to allow the defeat to ruin her confidence.

"No matter what happened that day, she won't beat me again at [the Olympics]," Bonnie said at the time. "I still will win the gold medal."

Now it was time for the 1988 Olympics to begin. About 25 of Bonnie's family and friends, known as the Blair Bunch, made the trip to Calgary to cheer her on.

On the morning of the 500-meter race, Bonnie was nervous. She ate a peanut-butter-and-jelly sandwich (her favorite) to quiet her upset stomach. At the rink, the pressure mounted when Christa, skating two pairs ahead of Bonnie, bettered her own world record with a time of 39.12 seconds! Bonnie knew she would have to skate faster than she ever had before to win the gold medal.

When the gun sounded, Bonnie got off to a great

start. With Christa watching from the sidelines, Bonnie raced around the track with near-perfect form and crossed the finish line in 39.10 seconds. That was just two hundredths of a second ahead of Christa's time and a new world record! Several other racers competed after Bonnie, but none of them came close. The gold medal was hers!

Bonnie stepped onto the podium to receive her medal. As "The Star-Spangled Banner" was played, tears came to her eyes. All of her hard work, and the efforts of so many other people, had been rewarded.

Bonnie also earned a bronze medal in the 1,000 meters. She was the only American athlete to win more than one medal at the Games. She was given the honor of carrying the U.S. flag in the closing ceremonies.

When she returned to the U.S., Bonnie was invited to the White House to attend a dinner for the prime minister of Canada, Brian Mulroney. Bonnie is a warm person with a quick and bright smile, and she received offers to endorse various products. She would never have to worry about money for training again!

Winning Words

"There's always going to be some doubt that comes in every once in a while. You have to always try to find the positives. That's what I've always tried to focus on." — *Bonnie Blair*

In August 1988, Bonnie moved back to Butte, where she enrolled at Montana College of Mineral Science and Technology. She took mostly physical education and business courses. She cut back on her training and didn't race until November. Bonnie missed the first two events of the World Cup season, but she won the overall title at the 1989 World Sprint Championships.

That year, Bonnie also took on a new challenge — cycling. Several other speed skaters, including Christa Rothenburger, had successfully taken up the sport. Bonnie was good enough to make the U.S. Women's Cycling team, but she soon gave up the sport. "Learning something different was a challenge in itself," she said.

The year ended on a sad note, however, when Bonnie's father died on Christmas Day in 1989. He was 78 and had been battling cancer for two years.

Bonnie wanted to concentrate on being a college student, so she cut back even more on her training. But she still managed a second-place finish in the World Sprint Championships in 1990 and a third in 1991.

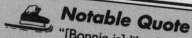 **Notable Quote**

"[Bonnie is] like Carl Lewis. She keeps going out and winning golds. . . . It took Dan Jansen 10 years to win one gold medal. She's won five. That tells you how great an athlete she is." — *Chantal Bailey, speed skater*

In the summer of 1991, Bonnie left college and returned to training full-time. "Doing other things in the years in between the Olympics was good both as a break and because it helped me realize I didn't want to look back and go, 'What if?' about 1992," she said.

Bonnie had her sights set on winning another gold medal at the 1992 Winter Olympics, which would be held in Albertville, France. She quickly showed that she was ready. In her first two World Cup events of the 1991–92 season, she won the 500- and 1,000-meter races. Bonnie arrived at the Olympics as the favorite in both events.

Once again, the Blair Bunch made the trip to the Games to support her. Once again, Bonnie calmed her prerace jitters with a peanut-butter-and-jelly sandwich. And once again, her major competition in the 500 was Christa Rothenburger Luding. (She had married.) A new-comer, Ye Qiaobo [YAY CHAH-bo] of China, was also very good. But Bonnie held them both off to win her second straight Olympic gold medal in the 500 meters. She dedicated the race to her father.

Four days later, Bonnie won the 1,000 meters. It wasn't easy: Her time was just two hundredths of a second faster than Ye Qiaobo's. With two gold medals (three overall), Bonnie was America's favorite winter-sports star.

Bonnie became known around the world. Her picture appeared on a cereal box, and the small Caribbean nation of Saint Vincent and the Northern Grenadines put her likeness on a postage stamp!

But being famous isn't always fun. "Just trying to go to the grocery store when all you need is a loaf of bread and a gallon of milk," Bonnie says. "And you wind up signing 10 autographs. That's when it gets difficult, when you're in a hurry to do something."

The next Winter Games were set for 1994 in Lillehammer, Norway. When the time came, the Blair Bunch traveled to Norway and Bonnie set her sights on repeating her double victory of 1992. She also hoped to set a couple of records in the process.

In the 500, Bonnie and her new coach, Nick Thometz, thought she could break her own world record of 39.10 if she could cover the first 100 meters in 10.5 seconds. She just missed, clocking a 10.6 for the first 100. Bonnie didn't break the record, but she won the gold medal anyway.

In the 1,000, Bonnie set her mind on breaking the track record of 1:19.97. For the longer race, her strategy was to get to 600 meters quickly and then hang on the rest of the way.

Skating in the second pair, Bonnie set the pace for the other competitors. She beat the track record by finishing in 1:18.74.

"I don't know if that's good enough," she told Coach Thometz as the two hugged after the race, "but that's all I had."

It was all Bonnie needed. She won the 1,000 by 1.38 seconds over the second-fastest skater, the largest margin of victory ever in the event. With those two gold medals, Bonnie became the only United States woman in history to win five golds in Olympic competition in any sport, winter or summer.

After the 1,000, Bonnie stepped onto the podium to receive her gold medal. Her eyes filled with tears once more as "The Star-Spangled Banner" played. But this time they were tears of farewell. Bonnie planned to compete at the World Sprint Championships in Milwaukee, Wisconsin, in February 1995, and then retire. She knew that this Olympic moment would never be repeated.

As Bonnie took a victory lap in the Olympic arena with the gold medal draped around her neck, she heard the Blair Bunch cheering, and laughed out loud. This was no time for tears. ★

TRAILBLAZER: ANNE HENNING

Anne Henning of Northbrook, Illinois, was the first United States woman to win an Olympic gold medal in speed skating. Anne won the 500-meters at the 1972 Games in Sapporo, Japan — when she was only 16 years old. The event has been won by Americans in four of the six Olympics since her win. Anne also won a bronze medal in the 1,000-meters.

Teresa Edwards

Mildred Edwards should have known early on that her daughter, Teresa, would become a sports star. Whenever the two of them went to church, Teresa would always try to outsing her mother. Talk about being competitive!

Growing up with four brothers in the tiny town of Cairo [KAY-ro], Georgia, Teresa was always playing a sport — softball at the playground, touch football in the street, track and field in the park, or basketball with an old bicycle wheel rim nailed to a pine tree in the front yard of their home.

Ms. Edwards thought her daughter was wasting her time, but Teresa practiced basketball endlessly. She had talent, and she wouldn't give up.

Because there is no professional basketball league for women in the United States, Teresa's name is not as well known as some

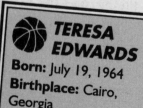

TERESA EDWARDS
Born: July 19, 1964
Birthplace: Cairo, Georgia
Height: 5' 11"
Weight: 155 pounds

A scorer, a playmaker, and a defensive stopper, Teresa is the first U.S. basketball player — male or female — to play on three Olympic teams.

other female athletes. But among those who follow the sport in college, the Olympics, and overseas, Teresa has become known as the "Michael Jordan of women's basketball."

★

Teresa and her mother have always been close. Ms. Edwards gave birth to Teresa when she was only 16 years old. Although Teresa's mother and father, Leroy Copeland, never married and never lived together, they had four more children, all boys. Mr. Copeland helped out financially, and Teresa's mother took any job she could get, eventually working as a machine operator in a bearings manufacturing plant in Cairo.

Teresa and her mother shared a bedroom in their house. They would talk about life for hours. Over the years, Ms. Edwards gave Teresa many words of wisdom.

"If you're not going to do it right — and do it hard — don't do it at all," she told Teresa more than once.

When Teresa was in the seventh grade at Washington Middle School in Cairo, she asked her mother for permission to try out for the girls' basketball team. Ms. Edwards refused. She thought Teresa should spend her time on something more constructive. But Teresa would not take no for an answer.

"She kept coming home late from school and laying it off on some teacher: 'I'm helping Miss So-and-so,'" Mildred Edwards once recalled. "Then one day she said, 'I need a new pair of sneakers because I made the team.' I said, 'Girl, you can't play basketball.' And Teresa said, 'Mama, I made the team.'"

Still her mother didn't believe it, until she went to see a game. Teresa was the best player on the court. She was faster than the other girls and could shoot better.

"I was quickly convinced," Ms. Edwards recalls. "I never missed a game after that."

In high school, Teresa was a sensation in basketball and track. She was named a high school all-American in basketball and led Cairo High to a second-place finish in the 1980 Georgia state high school track meet. At that meet, Teresa won the high jump, finished third in the 440-yard dash, and ran anchor on two relay teams that earned points.

★

Teresa's basketball skills earned her a scholarship to the University of Georgia. During her four years at Georgia, she averaged 15.5 points and 5.1 assists per game, and led the team to three straight Southeastern Conference

Winning Ways

Teresa earned all-American honors at the University of Georgia (1985–86). She was a member of the gold-medal-winning U.S. Olympic teams in 1984 and 1988, the gold-medal-winning U.S. world championship teams in 1986 and 1990, and the gold-medal-winning U.S. teams at Goodwill Games in 1986 and 1990.

championships. She became Georgia's all-time leader in assists (653) and steals (342), and was named to the all-American team in her junior and senior years. Teresa also worked toward a degree in recreation, which she received in 1989.

At 5' 11" and 155 pounds, Teresa had been a small forward at Cairo High, but she became a point guard in college. A point guard is the team's playmaker, the person who usually brings the ball upcourt and sets up the plays.

In 1984, when Teresa was a sophomore at Georgia, she was invited to try out for the U.S. Olympic team. She made it, but she was only 20 years old and was playing with and against far more experienced players. As a result, Teresa did not get to play often. She averaged only 2.5 points. The team won the gold medal, but the lack of playing time frustrated Teresa.

When she returned home to Cairo, the town of 8,000 renamed a street for her: Teresa Edwards Street. But Teresa felt unfulfilled by her Olympic experience.

Cool Fact

Teresa's hometown of Cairo, Georgia, was also the birthplace of Hall of Fame baseball player Jackie Robinson, the first African-American to play in the major leagues. Unlike Teresa, Jackie did not grow up in Cairo. His family moved to Pasadena, California, when Jackie was very young.

· Another college sophomore, Cheryl Miller of the University of Southern California, had turned out to be the star of the Olympic team. Unlike Teresa, Cheryl was a big scorer.

Scoring was not Teresa's main concern in college. She was more interested in bringing the ball upcourt and guarding the opponent's best guard or small forward. Only when the game was on the line did you notice that she was something special. Teresa earned a reputation of being at her best when the game was close.

"You'll see a different fire in her eyes, a different zeal in her game [when the game is close]," Georgia coach Andy Landers once said. "If a game gets close, she'll take it over."

One memorable game came against Long Beach State during the 1985 National Collegiate Athletic Association tournament. Georgia had been ahead by 18 points, but Long Beach State cut the lead to 10.

"I could see Teresa's burners start to kick in," recalled Coach Landers. "She couldn't get enough of anything — points, rebounds, anything.

Georgia got the ball to Teresa three times in a row and she scored each time. Georgia pulled away and won the game easily.

Despite her talent, Teresa often found herself in the shadow of Cheryl Miller during their college careers.

"My senior year, I was on the ballot for a lot of awards and I always finished second to Cheryl," Teresa says. "Every banquet I went to, I watched Cheryl get an award. It was a challenge. I wanted to get to where that person was."

★

In 1986, after her senior year of college, Teresa went to Italy to play professionally and polish her skills against international competition. Being such a long way from home helped make her mentally tough. Playing against some of the best players from other countries forced her to concentrate on playing her best every night.

Teresa was treated well, but she did not like it in Italy. She was homesick. She missed American television and American food.

"I'm bored to tears," Teresa said at the time. "I miss my family. I'm an American girl. I like hot dogs and fast food, not pizza. The people [in Europe] love you and respect you, but I hate it."

But the competition in Italy did help Teresa improve her game. In 1986, she led the U.S. women to victory against the Soviet Union in the title games of both the Goodwill Games and the world championships. In 1987, she averaged 17 points as the United States won the gold medal in the Pan American Games.

It wasn't until the 1988 Olympics, though, that Teresa finally earned a place in the spotlight. Cheryl had suffered a knee injury and did not make the team. That put the burden of carrying the team squarely on Teresa's shoulders.

Teresa responded by leading the team in steals (23) and assists (17), and scoring 16.6 points per game. With her all-around play, the U.S. won the gold medal again!

When she returned home to Cairo this time, Teresa was given a royal welcome by the town. A limousine met her car about 10 miles from town and she rode in style the rest of the way, accompanied by her family and a police escort. At a ceremony at town hall, she was presented with a new car. It was painted red and black — the University of Georgia's colors. The townspeople had raised the money to buy it. Even the local schoolchildren had chipped in.

Teresa was overwhelmed by the tribute. She longed to quit the Italian league and stay at home. But she was persuaded by the Italian team's president to give it one more try. Teresa was given a rent-free apartment and a $60,000 salary, but she stayed less than a month in Italy. She decided that being happy was more important than money. She returned to the University of Georgia to finish the 15 credits needed for her degree.

Winning Words

"I've come a long way, but if I went broke I'd be all right because I've been broke before. I'm not trying to be rich. Now if my family were rich and I had only a penny, then I'd be happy." — *Teresa Edwards*

"My mother didn't want me to go back to Italy either," Teresa says. "She knew how unhappy I was. She felt it was more important for me to finish school."

Teresa is tall and often wears her long black hair in braids. She is easily recognizable on the court and can dominate the action. But off the court she is humble and gracious.

"Someone of her stature, who is as good as she is, you'd expect to be more involved with herself," says Theresa Grentz, coach of the 1992 Olympic team. "Teresa's down-to-earth. She can't be bought. Values are important to her. Her humility and her simplicity of life make her very special to be around."

Teresa's humility also helps her put basketball in perspective. "My family is bigger to me than basketball," she says. "My attitude changed when I went overseas. I earned money so I could give something back to my mom. It's my turn to accept the responsibility of supporting her. What are you living for if you can't provide somebody with a better way of life? There's no mom like

Notable Quote

"Teresa is the greatest competitor ever to lace up a pair of basketball shoes. She may not beat you with her shooting or passing. But somehow, she will find a way to beat you." — *Coach Andy Landers of Georgia*

my mom. They don't make them like that anymore."

Teresa's desire to do something for her family forced her to reconsider her decision not to play overseas. After she received her college degree, she was prepared to accept a job in coaching or recreational work. But then a team that competes in a women's league in Japan offered Teresa $200,000 a year! She could not pass on the opportunity at earning that much money and she took the offer — even though the team is located in Nagoya, Japan, some 7,000 miles away from Cairo, Georgia.

Teresa had matured a great deal since her days in Italy and she found Japan easier to handle. "The movies are in English and the grocery store food is more like ours," she says. Teresa has learned a little Japanese but she usually uses an interpreter to communicate with her teammates.

Teresa was an immediate hit in Japan. She played forward and guard and averaged nearly 32 points and five assists a game in 1989–90, her first season. Her teammates were impressed. "Teresa plays like she has eyes in the back of her head," says Naomi Nakamura, the team captain.

★

In 1992, after the Japanese league season ended, Teresa returned to the United State to play for the U.S. Olympic team (again!). The U.S. had put together what many experts thought was the strongest women's team in history and they were expected to win the gold medal easily.

In the semifinal round, the U.S. was matched against the Unified Team, a squad of players from the former Soviet Union. Teresa and her teammates were not at their best that day.

The U.S. trailed, 47–41, at halftime but went ahead, 57–55, with 12 minutes 39 seconds left in the game. It looked as if they were on their way to victory. But they couldn't shoot straight. They missed five free throws and several close-in field goal attempts in the last five minutes. The Unified Team won the game, 79–73, and went on to win the gold medal. The U.S. finished third.

Teresa was disappointed by the loss, but not completely devastated. "It was one of the best teams I've played on," she says. "Just because we lost doesn't make it a bad summer. A bronze medal is good, too."

★

After the Olympics, Teresa returned to play in Japan. Then she joined a league in Spain for the 1993–94 season, playing for a team in Valencia, Spain. At the end of the Spanish season, Teresa joined the U.S. team for the world championships.

The U.S. team was upset again, this time by Brazil. But Teresa was one of the best players in the tournament. She averaged 12.7 points and 3.0 assists per game.

Teresa is undecided about whether or not to try out for the 1996 Olympic team. She is already the first U.S. basketball player, male or female, to play in three Olympics. She says she is taking it "one year at a time."

Teresa will continue to play in Europe for a while, but her long-range goal is to become a college coach. She also hopes to see the day when U.S. women basketball stars won't have to leave home to play professionally.

"By the time I'm established [as a coach], I hope there will be a women's pro league in the U.S. that I can coach in," she says.

No matter what league she coaches in, Teresa's talent and competitive fire is sure to make her, and those around her, winners. That same competitive spirit that Teresa showed during those Sunday mornings in church with her mom have helped make her into one of the greatest female athletes around. ★

TRAILBLAZER: ANN MEYERS

Ann Meyers was a star on the first U.S. women's basketball team to play in the Olympics (1976). The U.S. team won the silver medal. (Her brother, David, was an all-American at UCLA and later played with the Milwaukee Bucks.) Ann received all-American honors for all four of her years at UCLA. She was the first player drafted by the professional Women's Basketball League. She was also the first woman to sign an NBA contract, with the Indiana Pacers in 1979, but never played in a game. After she retired, Ann married Hall of Fame baseball pitcher Don Drysdale.

Nancy Lopez

Pretend you are writing a script for a movie. It's about a girl who excels at golf, but is not allowed to play on the nicest golf course in town because she is Mexican-American.

The girl doesn't give up. She practices on the run-down public golf course and becomes so good that she wins tournaments before she is a teenager. She wins a golf scholarship to college, then joins the women's professional golf tour and instantly becomes a star.

After a time, she falls in love with a major league baseball player. He becomes a World Series hero and she makes the golf Hall of Fame.

Now try to sell your script. If the people in Hollywood think it's farfetched, tell them it's all true. Call it *The Nancy Lopez Story.*

Nancy Lopez was born in Torrance, California, in 1957, but she was raised

NANCY LOPEZ
Born: January 6, 1957
Birthplace: Torrance, California
Height: 5' 4 ¼"
Weight: 130 pounds

Nancy made herself into a great golfer, and her enthusiasm made her a star. She is the youngest player ever to reach the LPGA Hall of Fame.

in the town of Roswell, New Mexico. Roswell is located about 100 miles north of the Texas border, near the Pecos River. Nancy was the younger of two daughters born to Domingo and Marina Lopez. Nancy's sister, Delma, is 12 years older than Nancy.

Both of Nancy's parents were of Mexican descent, although they were born in the United States. Mr. Lopez came from a family of nine that owned a cotton farm in Valentine, Texas. He never got past the third grade, but he learned all about cars and became an auto mechanic.

As a kid, Mr. Lopez had been a very good baseball player, and was once offered a contract with a minor-league team. He turned it down because the salary wasn't enough to support a family.

At the age of 40, Mr. Lopez fell in love with golf. He played at a public course because that was the only place Mexican-Americans were welcomed. Sometimes, Mrs. Lopez would play with her husband and, once in a while, little Nancy would tag along, too.

One day, when Nancy was 8, Mr. Lopez pulled a golf club out of his wife's bag and handed it to his daughter. Then he pointed to the ball.

"Hit it," he said. "You just keep on hitting until you get that ball into the hole. Stay just in back of us, little one, but try to keep up, too."

Every time Nancy swung, the ball soared over her parents' head. She used a wooden club called a driver for every shot, teeing the ball up no matter where it lay. It took time, but Nancy finally got the ball to the green. She then was allowed to take a shot with her mother's putter.

Nancy was hooked on the sport right away, and her parents were amazed at the way she could hit a golf ball. They did their best to encourage her. Her mother gave up the game so that there would be more money for Nancy to play. She wouldn't let Nancy wash the dishes for fear the water might hurt her hands and she wouldn't be able to swing the club!

Within a year of the day that Nancy first swung a club, she was entered in a Pee Wee tournament for girls between the ages of 8 and 12. Nine-year-old Nancy won the 27-hole event by 110 strokes!

Her father was so pleased that he bought Nancy a Barbie doll. From then on, each time Nancy won a tournament she got a Barbie doll. "I was so crazy about Barbie dolls that I never could get too many," Nancy wrote in her autobiography, *The Education of a Woman Golfer*.

Nancy soon had a roomful of dolls. She was a phenomenon as an amateur golfer, winning the New Mexico

Winning Ways

Nancy won 9 tournaments in her first full year (1978) on the Ladies' Professional Golf Association (LPGA) tour, including a record 5 in a row. She won the LPGA Championship three times, and won 47 tournaments from 1978–93.

Women's Amateur championship when she was only 12, and two more times after that! She won the U.S. Junior Girls' championship twice and the Mexican Amateur once. In high school, Nancy played on the boys' golf team. At age 16, she qualified to play in her first U.S. Women's Open.

As good a golfer as she was, Nancy still managed to enjoy a normal life as a high school student. She was active in swimming, basketball, track, gymnastics, the Girl Scouts, and a girls' club called "Chums."

Her best friend in high school was a Mexican-American but many of her friends were Anglos, as the white Americans were called. Still, she had firsthand experience of how it feels to be discriminated against because of your race. She dated a boy whose parents objected to her because she was Mexican-American. And although she was possibly the best golfer in town, she was not allowed to play on the fine golf course at the local country club because she was Mexican-American. That made it harder for Nancy to improve her game.

 Cool Fact

As a teenager, Nancy had the nickname "Skeetch." That was given to her by her friends because of the screeching noise the tires on her canary yellow 1972 Gran Torino made when she drove it off quickly.

The only course in town on which Nancy was allowed to play was not well cared for. It was a nine-hole course and did not have enough sand traps to make it challenging. The greens also were not watered regularly, making the grass very dry and causing the ball to move much faster. The best thing about it was it cost only $1.25 to play. After Nancy became the state amateur champion, the mayor of Roswell gave her free golf privileges on a better public course.

Nancy never had any lessons and her swing was considered strange by some golf experts. Nancy uses a very slow backswing. She does this to make sure the clubface will be square when it hits the ball. Unlike most golfers, she doesn't turn her hips very much and she keeps her left heel on the ground during her backswing. Nancy's follow-through also raises eyebrows. She sweeps the clubface all the way through the ball and ends with the club wrapped around her shoulders and her entire body facing the target.

Nancy once asked men's golf champion Lee Trevino, also a Mexican-American, if she should change her swing. Lee didn't even ask to see it. "You can't argue with success," he told her. "If you swing badly but still score well and win, don't change a thing."

Nancy sure scored well. After high school, the University of Tulsa (Oklahoma) offered her a golf scholarship. She attended school for two years, studying engineering and business. In 1975, her freshman year, she played in the U.S. Open as an amateur, and tied two pros for second place. In 1976, her sophomore year, she won the national college women's championship. After that year, she left college to join the pro tour. She was 20.

"I felt like I had no other place to go [in college golf]," she once said. "I needed to go forward and set other goals, reach the highest point of my whole career."

It didn't take Nancy long to establish herself on the Ladies' Professional Golf Association (LPGA) tour. Her first event as a pro, in July 1977, was the important U.S. Women's Open, and she finished second. She was second in her next two tournaments as well, before a hand injury forced her to miss a few weeks of play.

Then, tragedy struck Nancy's life: Her mother died following an appendix operation. Nancy left the tour, but after a few weeks she returned, vowing to win her first tournament as a tribute to her mother.

And did she win! Nancy's first victory came in Florida in the Bent Tree Classic in February 1978. Two weeks later, she won the Sunstar Classic in Los Angeles, California. Then, beginning in May, Nancy won four tournaments in a row to tie an LPGA record.

On June 16, Nancy entered the Bankers Trust Classic in Rochester, New York, going for her fifth straight win. It would be one of the most exciting matches of her career.

On the first round of the three-day, 54-hole tournament (18 holes each day), Nancy teed off on the

10th hole, and watched her drive sail into a crowd of fans and hit a spectator on the head. Nancy rushed over to the man and burst into tears when she saw him lying on the ground with blood on his forehead. The man said he was okay, but Nancy was still crying as she walked down the fairway. She double-bogeyed the hole. Nancy finished the round with a 72, and the next day posted a 73. Those were not scores that would win a tournament on this par-73 course. *(For golf terms, see How It Works, page 95.)*

Entering the final round, Nancy trailed leader Jane Blalock. But under pressure, Nancy was able to lift her play to a higher level. She birdied the first hole. She scored another birdie on the fourth hole, and did it again on the eighth. On the ninth hole, she sank a 25-foot putt for still another birdie.

In the earlier rounds, Nancy had not played well on the back nine, bogeying several holes. But now at each of those holes she said to herself, "You owe me one." She played with the confidence of a true champion.

Nancy reached the 17th green tied with Jane

Winning Words

"When you're behind in a tournament is when you charge. You have to gamble. I'd rather wind up fifth in a tournament because I took a chance to try to finish first, even though I might have finished second by playing it safe." — *Nancy Lopez*

Blalock for the lead. She needed to sink a long, 35-foot putt for a birdie and the lead. The putt was a tough one. However, another golfer sank a similar putt moments before it was Nancy's turn to putt. Nancy learned something about the roll of the green from that shot. She took a deep breath, hit her putt strong, and showed off her broadest smile when the ball went into the hole!

Nancy finished with a 4-under-par 69 — and the lead. Then she sat down on her club bag and waited for Jane to finish. When Jane's third shot went past the pin, making a tie impossible, Nancy jumped up and began to cry tears of joy. She had accomplished something no other golfer on the LPGA tour had ever done. She had won five tournaments in a row!

Nancy finished her rookie season with nine tournament victories. She was named LPGA Player of the Year and Rookie of the Year, and was awarded the Vare Trophy for having the lowest scoring average on the tour. Nancy was 21 and she was on top of the golfing world.

Crowds loved her for her charisma and her thrilling come-from-behind ability. Sports reporters found that Nancy was not only a remarkable golfer but a very special person as well. She was charming and polite, and always was willing to discuss her game.

Even her opponents were fans. "Nancy has been a tremendous draw and has focused nationwide attention on the tour, which is something we have all wanted," veteran golfer and Hall of Famer Carol Mann explained. "In addition to all this, she happens to be a dear person."

Jane Blalock agreed. "There hasn't been a Nancy Lopez before," Jane said. "No one even close."

Nancy's second full year on the tour, 1979, was almost as brilliant as her first. In April, on her 22nd birthday, she married Tim Melton, a sportscaster she had met at a tournament. Then, Nancy won 8 of the 19 tournaments she entered, and Player of the Year honors again.

Although Nancy won three tournaments in each of the next two seasons, her life off the course was not so successful. All the travel and time away from home began to hurt her marriage.

Nancy found a friend she could talk to about her problems. He was Ray Knight, a major league baseball player. Ray had met Nancy when he was playing for the Cincinnati Reds and her husband, Tim, was working for a Cincinnati television station. Later, Ray was traded to

How It Works

Par is the number of shots or strokes a good player should use to hit the ball from the tee into the hole. A par-3 hole should take three strokes, a par-4 hole four strokes, and so on. A score of one-under-par is called a **birdie**. A score of two-under-par is an **eagle**. A score of one-over-par on a hole is called a **bogey**. Two strokes over is a **double-bogey**.

the Houston Astros and Tim took a job as a sportscaster in Houston.

One day, Nancy asked Ray over for a cup of cocoa and told him that she was considering divorcing Tim. Ray was surprised at the news but he offered his support. "He was really my only friend during that period when I was struggling the most," Nancy said later.

After Nancy and Tim separated in 1981, she and Ray talked to each other a lot, on the telephone and in person. Gradually, they became more than friends. Nancy divorced Tim early in 1982, and she and Ray began dating in March. Seven months later, they were married.

In 1983, the Knights had their first child, Ashley Marie. Nancy cut back on her playing so she could stay at home and care for her family as much as possible.

TRAILBLAZER: MICKEY WRIGHT

Mickey Wright was one of the first big stars of women's golf. She took up the sport at age of 11. She won the national junior title in 1952 at 16, turned pro at 18, and in 1963 won 13 tournaments on the women's tour. She won 82 LPGA tournaments during her 25-year career, including the USGA Open (now the U.S. Women's Open) and the LPGA championship four times each. She was named Woman Athlete of the Year by the Associated Press in 1963 and 1964.

But Ray was convinced that Nancy could be Number 1 on the tour again, and gave her a pep talk. She increased her schedule to 25 tournaments in 1985 and took Ashley and a nanny with her on the tour. She won five tournaments, including the LPGA Championship for the second time, and did finish the year ranked first!

Meanwhile, Ray's baseball career was falling apart. He suffered a series of injuries with the Astros and, with his career all but over, was traded to the New York Mets.

Nancy and Ray had another daughter, Erinn Shea, in 1986, and Ray's fortunes on the field greatly improved. The Mets beat the Boston Red Sox in the World Series and Ray was named the Series' Most Valuable Player.

Things have continued to go well for Ray and Nancy. Nancy won her 35th LPGA tournament in 1987 to qualify for the Hall of Fame at age 30 — the youngest player in history to do so.

A third daughter, Torri Heather, arrived in 1991. Nancy continued to balance golf and home life. She did not play every week, but she won at least one tournament each year. Ray retired after the 1988 season and became a sportscaster. He joined the Reds as a coach in 1994.

Of course, *The Nancy Lopez Story* isn't over yet. Ray hopes to manage in the big leagues someday and Nancy is still in pursuit of more golfing titles. But for now, it looks like this movie has a happy ending. ★

Shannon Miller

I t all started with a gift that 5-year-old Shannon Miller and her 7-year-old sister, Tessa, received from their parents for Christmas in 1982: a trampoline!

But when Shannon and Tessa began bouncing on the trampoline and doing flips, Mr. and Mrs. Miller became scared that some terrible accident might happen to one of them. No more trampoline, they insisted.

Instead, the Millers signed up their daughters for gymnastics at the club in their hometown of Edmond, Oklahoma. Little did they know that Shannon would one day turn out to be a world champion.

★

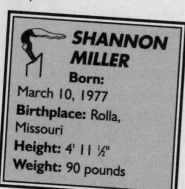

SHANNON MILLER
Born: March 10, 1977
Birthplace: Rolla, Missouri
Height: 4' 11 ½"
Weight: 90 pounds

From the time she started gymnastics, Shannon Miller showed a special talent for the sport. She is generally a quiet person, but she was aggressive in her gymnastics routines. She paid close attention to

Shannon was the smallest member of the 1992 U.S. Summer Olympic team, but she won more medals — five — than anyone else on the team.

her coach and always wanted to try harder routines. She had a fierce drive to perform well.

Shannon's mother, Claudia, works as a bank vice president, but she became a gymnastics judge in her spare time. (Her father, Ron, is a physics professor at the University of Central Oklahoma.)

When Shannon was 8, she and her mother visited the Soviet Union with Shannon's gymastics club. The Soviets had dominated international gymnastics competition for 40 years. Their coaches were considered the world's best. (Beginning in 1991, the Soviet Union broke up into 15 separate countries.)

One of the Soviet coaches thought Shannon had a lot of potential. He told Mrs. Miller that Shannon would need excellent coaching to develop her talent properly.

When Shannon and her mom returned home, Shannon enrolled at a club called Dynamo Gymnastics in Oklahoma City, which is about 45 minutes from Edmond. The coach at Dynamo was Steve Nunno.

Coach Nunno had been an assistant coach with Bela Karolyi, the most famous coach in gymnastics.

Winning Ways

Shannon won five medals at the 1992 Summer Olympics. She is the only U.S. woman to win two all-around titles at the World Gymnastics Championships (1993 and 1994).

Coach Karolyi had trained Olympic gold medalists Nadia Comaneci and Mary Lou Retton. Coach Nunno hoped to set up his own Olympic training ground in Oklahoma City.

Coach Nunno saw Shannon's potential right away. Shannon had been doing difficult routines for quite a while, so the coach let her train with his older and more experienced gymnasts. He knew that working with the older kids would help Shannon learn faster.

Training under Coach Nunno is not easy. He is very demanding. When he works with his elite, or top, gymnasts, Coach Nunno will walk from apparatus to apparatus as more than 20 girls go through their routines. He seems to have eyes in the back and on the sides of his head. He will be watching a gymnast perform a vault, then turn and shout "That's not good enough" across the gym if he doesn't like the floor exercise routine another gymnast is performing.

Under Coach Nunno, Shannon developed into one of the top junior-level gymnasts in the United States. When she was 11, she went to the Junior Pan American Games, a competition for young athletes from all the countries in North and South America, and finished second in the all-around competition. A year later, she won the uneven bars at the U.S. Olympic Festival.

At age 13, Shannon became a member of the U.S. national team! At the 1991 world championships, she helped the U.S. win the silver medal in the team

competition. She also placed sixth in the all-around, qualified for all four event finals (balance beam, vault, uneven
bars, and floor exercise), and won a silver medal on the
bars. *(For more on competition, see How It Works, page 104.)*

★

Coach Nunno and U.S. Olympic coach Peggy Liddick
were grooming Shannon for the 1992 Olympics. She had
been making steady progress in her performances, and
they felt she would be ready to shine by then. But then
something happened that nearly destroyed their plans.

During a training session, Shannon injured her
elbow and needed surgery. That set Shannon's training
back, but she made a spectacular recovery. Just nine
weeks after the injury, she competed at the U.S. Olympic
Trials and earned a place on the U.S. team.

The 1992 Summer Olympics were being held in
Barcelona, Spain. Going into the Games, Shannon was
not the star of the U.S. gymnastics team. That honor
belonged to Kim Zmeskal. Kim had won the 1992 all-
around world championship, and her coach, Bela Karolyi,
had high hopes for her winning a gold medal.

But the pressure of competing in the Olympics
proved to be too much for Kim. She was nervous, and fell
doing a routine on the balance beam. It was a move she
said she couldn't remember ever missing, even in practice.

After Kim's failure, the competition was wide open.
Shannon was determined to do well. "Other people may
not have had high expectations for me in Barcelona," she

said later, "but I had high expectations for myself."

Shannon was in fourth place in the all-around competition entering the vault — her final event. The leader was Tatiana Gutsu, who was competing for the Unified Team of athletes from the former Soviet Union.

A graceful gymnast who is surprisingly powerful, Shannon excels in the uneven bars and the balance beam but sometimes has problems with the vault. As she stepped onto the mat, Shannon felt nervous for the first time in the competition. Then she began sprinting down the runway. She hit the takeoff board and launched into a spectacular, twisting vault, called a Yurchenko layout with a full twist. The judges awarded her a score of 9.975 out of a possible 10. Shannon had vaulted into first place!

Now it was Tatiana's turn to try to recapture the lead. Each vaulter gets two attempts. The score on Tatiana's first vault was not enough to overtake Shannon. But on her second attempt, she concentrated even more, raced down the runway, and executed the vault she needed — for a score of 9.950. Tatiana won the gold medal

Winning Words

"It's hard to think of gymnastics as fun when you're working out eight hours a day. But when you get to a competition, you're having fun. I work hard because that's where I want to be." — Shannon Miller

and Shannon ended up with the silver.

Shannon also won a silver medal in the balance beam and a bronze medal in the floor exercise in the individual competition. She won another bronze medal when the United States placed third in the team competition.

Shannon had won five Olympic medals! At 4' 6"and 69 pounds, she was the shortest and lightest U.S. athlete at the Games. But she had won more medals than any of her teammates.

Shannon returned to the United States as a star. She was made honorary mayor of Oklahoma City and honorary

How It Works

Female gymnasts compete in four events: the vault, uneven bars, balance beam, and floor exercise. In the Olympics, competitions are divided into three parts. On the first two days, all gymnasts perform routines on all four pieces of apparatus. Their scores are then used to determine the winners of the team event. (There is no team event at the world championships.) The 36 gymnasts who score the highest combined individual scores move on to the all-around finals, in which they once again compete on each apparatus. The gymnast with the highest point total after all four events is the all-around winner. The top eight scorers on each apparatus, based on their combined scores from the team and all-around finals, move on to the apparatus finals. Medals are awarded for each individual apparatus, too.

governor of Oklahoma! She was given a new car — even though she was 15 and still too young to drive.

Suddenly, Shannon was receiving more than 100 fan letters a week and being showered with gifts from admirers. When a team of Olympic and world-champion gymnasts gave a series of exhibitions in 23 U.S. cities, Shannon received the loudest cheers.

But Shannon's fans hadn't seen the best of her yet. As soon as she returned from the tour, Shannon was back in the gym every day, getting ready for the World Gymnastics Championships in Birmingham, England. Her goal was to win the world all-around title.

Shannon works out 6 ½ hours every weekday. She is at the gym by 7 a.m., works out until 8:30 a.m., and then goes to school. After school, she trains from 4 p.m. until 9 p.m. On Saturdays, she works out from 9 a.m. until 1 p.m.

Shannon arrived in Birmingham as the gymnast to beat. "If anybody beat Shannon," said Coach Nunno, "she was going to beat herself."

Shannon was not about to do that. Once again she had to come from behind in the all-around competition. She had scored well in the uneven bars but done poorly on the balance beam. She was in fifth place entering the floor exercise, but scored a 9.825 in that event to move back into contention for the gold medal.

Now, Shannon's shot at a championship came down to the vault. Coach Nunno had a tough decision to make: Should he have Shannon try a double-twisting vault, which was worth a full 10 points, or a less difficult vault, with a full twist, that was worth 9.800 at most? The double-twist would lock up the gold medal if Shannon performed it well. If she didn't, though, she could lose any shot at winning the title.

Coach Nunno decided on the full twist and Shannon performed both her vaults beautifully. She scored 9.775 on one vault and a perfect 9.800 on the other. Shannon won the world title by only .007 points!

While in Birmingham, Shannon came down with an upset stomach, which slowed her down in the individual apparatus competition. She had to drop out of the vault competition and fell off the balance beam twice in that competition. But she was able to bounce back to win gold medals in the uneven bars and the floor exercise.

It wasn't a bad encore to her Olympic performance. Shannon could now officially claim the title as the world's greatest gymnast!

A year later, Shannon returned to the world championships, which were being held in Brisbane, Australia. She was trying to become the first U.S. gymnast to win back-to-back all-around championships.

It would be an uphill battle. Shannon had injured a stomach muscle a month earlier and had missed two weeks of training. But once again, Shannon rose to the challenge. She entered the final event — the vault — needing to score 9.775 to win the title. She scored 9.812

and won her second straight world championship! She also added a gold medal in the individual balance beam competition.

The day after returning from the world championships, Shannon was back at the Dynamo gym, training hard. "Shannon is the most dedicated individual you'll ever meet," Coach Nunno said.

★

There were many demands on Shannon's time now. She was photographed for a fashion magazine. She attended Oklahoma's Shannon Miller Appreciation Day and went to a celebration for former U.S. Presidents Richard Nixon, Gerald Ford, Ronald Reagan, and George Bush.

Shannon, however, would much rather play with her dog, Dusty, than make public appearances. She is a homebody by nature. She likes to sew her own clothes, or just sit around the house and watch television, or listen to music — especially music from the 1960's and 1970's.

Being famous has not changed Shannon. "I still go

Cool Fact

Shannon's dog, Dusty, is part golden retriever and part Labrador. He loves to go running with Shannon and her mom at the University of Central Oklahoma track near their home. And Shannon loves it when her parents bring Dusty to the airport to greet her after a big meet!

to public school, I still work out, my coach still yells at me in the gym," she says. "My brother [Troy, who is four years younger] and sister still pick on me and I still pick on them. Many of my friends have known me since I was in the first grade and they still treat me the same. I've never been accused of being big-headed."

How about eggheaded? Despite her many travels and long practice sessions, Shannon maintains a straight-A average at Edmond North Mid High School. Even when she is away, she gets her studying and homework done. While Shannon was at the world championships in Australia in April 1994, her high school Spanish teacher faxed her an exam. Shannon completed it and faxed it back. She got an A!

TRAILBLAZER: CATHY RIGBY

The first giant of American women's gymnastics was 4' 11" Cathy Rigby from Long Beach, California. Cathy competed for the United States at the 1968 Olympics in Mexico City at age 16. Two years later, she won a silver medal on the balance beam at the world championships in Yugoslavia. At the time, it was the best finish ever by an American female gymnast. Cathy also competed in the 1972 Olympics in Munich, Germany. She later became an actress and starred in a Broadway production of *Peter Pan*.

"I don't have much time for homework, with all the training, but somehow I make the time," she says. "I've learned through gymnastics that you can't wait until the last minute. I don't know if I'd be making straight A's if it weren't for the discipline I got from gymnastics."

"She's an achiever," says Shannon's dad. "She wants to do well in gymnastics, graduate with her class at school, and make straight A's."

The Miller family has supported Shannon throughout her quest for success. And they are all into gymnastics. Shannon's brother, Troy, tied for the gold medal in the floor exercise at the Level 6 Oklahoma State meet when he was 12 years old. Tessa, who is two years older than Shannon, has coached kids in gymnastics.

The next Olympics are coming up in 1996. They will be held in Atlanta, Georgia. Shannon may be there, or she may not. "I hadn't planned to keep competing until '96," said Shannon. "but after the '92 Olympics were over, I didn't want to stop. It's so much fun!"

Meanwhile, Shannon has plenty to do. She wants to go to college. She is active in antidrug campaigns and the "Stay in School" and "Feed the Children" programs.

"People criticize Shannon, saying she has been programmed," says Coach Nunno. "And she is programmed. But she programs herself."

It has often been said that special things come in small packages. Shannon Miller is certainly proof of that. ★